Implementation of
RTI ACT 2005 in Armed Forces
and
Its Implications

Implementation of
RTI ACT 2005 in Armed Forces
and
Its Implications

By

Brig AK Vyas

Centre for Joint Warfare Studies (CENJOWS)

New Delhi

Vij Books India Pvt Ltd

New Delhi (India)

Published by

Vij Books India Pvt Ltd

(Publishers, Distributors & Importers)
2/19, Ansari Road, Darya Ganj
New Delhi - 110002
Phones: 91-11-43596460, 91-11- 47340674
Fax: 91-11-47340674
e-mail : vijbooks@rediffmail.com
web: www.vijbooks.com

ISBN: 978-93-82652-14-4

Contents

Foreword

It is indeed a privilege to write a foreword of the book on 'RTI Act 2005 and its Implications to the Armed Forces' by Brig AK Vyas. This book is written with the aim of understanding the intrinsic features of the Act and its impact on the functioning of Armed Forces. The attempt of the author to outline importance of the Right to Information Act 2005, which is empowering ordinary citizens to procure information from public authorities.

The right to information is to some extent enshrined in the Constitution of India Article 19 (1) (a) which states that every citizen has the freedom of speech and expression. The Supreme Court, in one of the case stated that people cannot express themselves unless they are in possession of appropriate information. Freedom of speech and expression, if exercised without information loses its strength.

Knowledge is power and the Right to Information Act 2005 has brought this power to people, without which no democracy can retain its intrinsic character, because in a vibrant democracy, citizens are the custodians of power. This Act takes citizenry beyond the power of exercising their franchise; it allows the taxpayer to see what is being dome with his money, giving him the chance to question Government. Laws, such as this, promote and ensure transparency.

Armed Forces have not been included in the second schedule of RTI Act which exempts few organisations from the purview of RTI Act 2005; hence RTI Act is also equally applicable to all three services of the Armed Forces being Central Government Organisations. It is undeniably credible to know that all three service headquarters of Ministry of Defence have adequately geared up to undertake challenges involved in processing of RTI cases. All three services have already established comprehensive

RTI mechanism at the headquarters and at subordinate formations and successfully meeting the aspirations of citizens of the country by provisioning permissible information held with them.

In this book, Col (now Brig) AK Vyas, a Senior Fellow at the Centre for Joint Warfare Studies has aptly covered nuances of the RTI Act and its implications to the Armed Forces. He has conceptualized and analysed the subject well and meticulously covered various illustrations and case studies supported with number of decisions of the Central Information Commission and its application to Armed Forces. These supplements have made this reading more interesting and will also act as a reference in future.

The research work undertaken by the Senior Fellow, has transformed into an informative, stimulating and interesting book which will not only enrich the knowledge of environment on the subject but will also offer as an apt guidelines for the organisations to further convalesce the procedures while dealing with RTI cases.

(KB Kapoor),
Maj Gen (Retd)
Director CENJOWS

Chapter 1
Introduction

Preamble

The Right to Information Act 2005 (RTI) is an Act of the Parliament of India " to provide for setting out the practical regime of right to information for citizens." The Act applies to all States and Union Territories of India except the State of Jammu and Kashmir. Jammu And Kashmir State has its own act called Jammu & Kashmir Right to Information Act, 2009. Under the provisions of the Act, any citizen may request for information from a "public authority"[1] which is required to reply expeditiously or within thirty days. The Act also requires every public authority to computerise their records for wide dissemination and to pro-actively publish certain categories of information so that the citizens need minimum recourse to request for information formally. This law was passed by parliament on 15 June 2005 and came fully into force on 12 October 2005. Information disclosure in India was hitherto restricted by the Official Secrets Act 1923 and various other special laws, which the new RTI Act now relaxes.

The RTI Laws were first successfully enacted by the state governments of Karnataka (2000), Goa (1997), Rajasthan (2000), Tamilnadu (1997), Delhi (2001), Maharashtra (2002), Assam (2002), Madhya Pradesh (2003), and Jammu and Kashmir (2004). The Maharashtra and Delhi State level enactments are considered to have been the most widely used.

---

1 A Body of Government or Instrumentality of State.

The Delhi RTI Act is still in force. Jammu & Kashmir has its own Right to Information Act of 2009, the successor to the repealed J&K Right to Information Act, 2004 and its 2008 amendments.

Right to Information Movement in India.

In early 1990s, Mazdoor Kisan Shakti Sangathana (MKSS) began a movement to − bring in transparency in village accounts. Initially, MKSS lobbied government to obtain information such as master rolls (employment and payment records) and bills and vouchers relating to purchase and transportation of materials. This information was then crosschecked at Jan Sunwais (public hearings) against actual testimonies of workers. The public hearings were incredibly successful in drawing attention to corruption and exposing leakages in the system. Success of MKSS became a source of inspiration for activists in India and led to the genesis of a broader discourse on the right to information in India. In 1993, a first draft RTI law was proposed by the Consumer Education and Research Council, Ahmedabad (CERC).

1. A Body of Government or Instrumentality of State

In 1996, the Press Council of India headed by Justice P B Sawant presented a draft model law on the right to information to the Government of India. The draft model law was later updated and renamed the PCI-NIRD Freedom of Information Bill 1997. MKSS's advocacy gave rise to the National Campaign on People's Right to Information (NCPRI), which was formed to advocate for the right to information at the national level. In 1997 efforts to legislate for the right to information, at both the State and National level, quickened. A working group under the chairmanship of Mr. H D Shourie (the Shourie Committee) was set up by the Central Government and given the mandate to prepare draft legislation on freedom of information. The Shourie Committee's Report and draft law were published in 1997. The Shourie Committee draft law was passed through two successive governments, but was never introduced in Parliament.

In 1999, during the NDA Government, then Union Minister for Urban Development, Mr Ram Jethmalani issued an administrative order enabling citizens to inspect and receive photocopies of files. Shourie Committee draft law was reworked into the Freedom of Information Bill 2000. It was passed in December 2002 and received Presidential asset on January 2003, as the Freedom of Information Act 2002.

In 1998, the Congress Party promised in its election manifesto to enact a law on right to information if it came to power while facing elections in the state of Rajasthan. Following their election, the Party appointed a committee of bureaucrats to draft a bill on the right to information. As the Committee was comprised only bureaucrats, strong objections were raised by civil society organisations, following which the members of MKSS and National Campaign for Peoples Right to Information were invited to assist in drafting the bill. MKSS and NCPRI conducted a host of consultations in each divisional Headquarters of the State. Drawing on the input from these consultations, a draft civil society Right to Information Bill was prepared, which was then submitted to the Committee. The Committee drew on the citizens draft Bill for its recommendations, but refused to accept the Bill in total. The Rajasthan Right to Information Act 2000 was eventually passed on 11 May 2000. The Act in its final form retained many of the suggestions of the RTI movement, but diluted others.

In the early 2000s Anna Hazare led a movement in Maharashtra state which forced the state government to pass a stronger Maharashtra Right to Information Act. This Act was later considered as the base document for the Right to Information Act 2005 (RTI), enacted by the Union Government. It also ensured that the President of India assented to this new Act. The state of Maharashtra – home to one of the world's largest cities, Mumbai, adopted a Right to Information Act in 2003, prodded by the hunger strike of prominent activist, Anna Hazare.

In 2004, under the leadership of Sonia Gandhi, the Congress party won the national elections and formed the Central Government. Aruna Roy was inducted into the National Advisory Committee (NAC), an extremely powerful but extra-constitutional quasi-governmental body headed by Sonia Gandhi which effectively supervises the working of the common minimum programme of UPA government. Aruna Roy submitted a paper recommending amendments to the 2002 Freedom of Information Act to the NAC which in turn sent by it to the Prime Minister's Office.

The Right to Information Bill 2004 (RTI Bill 2004) was tabled on 23 December during the winter session of the Lok Sabha. The RTI Bill

2004 was based largely on recommendations submitted to the Government by the NAC which was passed by the Indian parliament in 2005. On 20 July 2006 the Union Cabinet amended the Right to Information Act 2005 to exclude the file noting by the government officials from its purview. Hazare began his fast unto death on 9 August 2006 in Alandi against the proposed amendment. He ended his fast on 19 August 2006, after the government agreed to change its earlier decision.

Disclosure of State information in British India was governed from 1889   by the Official Secrets Act. This law secures information related to security of the State, sovereignty of the country and friendly relations with foreign states, and contains provisions which prohibit disclosure of non-classified information. Civil Service conduct rules and the Indian Evidence Act impose further restrictions on government officials' powers to disclose information to the public.

Freedom of Information Act 2002.

Passage of a national level law, however, proved to be a difficult task. Given the experience of state governments in passing practicable legislation, the Central Government appointed a working group under H. D. Shourie and assigned it the task of drafting legislation. The Shourie draft, in an extremely diluted form, was the basis for the Freedom of Information Bill, 2000 which eventually became law under the Freedom of Information Act, 2002. In late 2002 the Centre for Public Interest Litigation (CPIL) asked for scrutiny of the proposed bill by the Supreme Court to determine whether the bill gave citizens sufficient power to find out about governance. The government had been reluctant to recognize that the people had a right to know, and after the CPIL filing it rushed through the bill without correcting known defects. This Act was severely criticized for permitting too many exemptions, not only under the standard grounds of national security and sovereignty, but also for requests that would involve "disproportionate diversion of the resources of a public authority". There was no upper limit on the charges that could be levied. There were no penalties for not complying with a request for information. This Act, consequently, never came into effective force.

Act in its Present Form.

In order to promote transparency and accountability in administration, the Indian Parliament enacted the Freedom of Information Act, 2002, which was repealed later and a new act, The Right to Information Act, came into force on 12 October 2005. The new law empowers Indian citizens to seek information from a Public Authority, thus making the Government and its functionaries more accountable and responsible. The Act has now been in operation for over Five years and has benefited many, including the poor and the underprivileged. It has been highlighted in this report through various case studies that RTI Act has adequate "teeth" to bring in transparency and reduce corruption. At the same time it accepted that the Act has not yet reached the stage of implementation which was envisioned. However, it is still a matter of pride that we have given to ourselves, a tool which has the potential to usher in transparency, and reduce corruption. Notwithstanding the improvement required, the following achievements are undisputable:-

(a) The basic tenets of the Act have been implemented and the institutional mechanism is in place and is in use by citizens.

(b) The institution of Information Commission has assumed a pivotal position.

(c) Civil society organisations have been, and continue to be, active in ensuring the implementation of the Act in letter and spirit.

(d) Civil society organisations and the media have started using the Act for bringing in transparency and objectivity.

(e) Centre and State Government departments have initiated the training of key functionaries to assume the responsibilities of Public Information Officers and First   Appellate Authority.

(f) Government employees/Public Authorities are aware of the basic elements of the Act.

(g) Various State Governments have taken up initiatives, which go beyond the stipulations of the Act, and further the spirit of the Act.

Chapter 2

Salient Features of RTI Act 2005

Layout of RTI Act 05

It is an Act to provide for setting out the practical regime of right to information for citizens to secure access to information under the control of public authorities, in order to promote transparency and accountability in the working of every public authority. Chapter wise broad details of content are given as under:-

Chapter I

Section 1 gives out the short title, extent and commencement of the Act. It is noteworthy to mention that the Act extends to the whole of India except the state of J&K.

Section 2 lists out definitions of certain terms used in the Act.

Chapter II

Chapter II of the Act encompasses following sections:-

(a) **Section 3** specifies subject to the provisions of this Act, all citizens shall have the right to information.

(b) **Section 4** lays down the obligations of the Public Authorities.

(c) **Section 5** deals with the designation and duties of Central Public Information Officers/Public Information Officers.

(d) **Section 6** lays down the procedure to be followed by an applicant for requesting information.

(e) **Section 7** gives out the action to be taken by the Central Public Information Officers/Public Information Officers for disposal of requests for information.

(f) **Sections 8 & 9** list out information which is exempt from disclosure under the Act and grounds for rejection to access in certain cases, respectively.

(g) **Section 10** gives out the severability clause under which access may be provided to that part of the record which does not contain any information which is exempt from disclosure under this Act and which can be reasonably severed from any record that contains exempt information.

(h) **Section 11** lays down the procedure for sharing information pertaining to a third party.

Chapter III

Chapter III of the act primarily deals with Central Information Commission and has following sections:-

(a) **Section 12** deals with the constitution of the Central Information Commission.

(b) **Section 13** lays down the term of office and conditions of service of the Chief Information Commissioner or Information Commissioner.

(c) **Section 14** lays down the conditions and procedure for removal of the Chief Information Commissioner or Information Commissioner.

Chapter IV

Chapter IIV of the act defines setting up of State Information Commission and has following sections:-

(a) **Section 15** deals with constitution of State Information Commission (SIC).

(b) **Section 16** lays down the term of office and conditions of service of the State Chief Information Commissioner or State Information Commissioner.

(c) **Section 17** lays down the conditions and procedure for removal of the State Chief Information Commissioner or State Information Commissioner.

Chapter V

This chapter deals with the powers and functions of the Information Commissions, appeals and penalties and has following sections and sub-sections:-

(a) **Section 18** lists out the powers and functions of Information Commissions.

    (i) **Sub Section 18** (1) states that subject to the provisions of this Act, it shall be the duty of the Central Information Commission, to receive and inquire into a complaint from any person.

    (ii) **Sub Section 18** (2) states that where the Central Information Commissioner, is satisfied that there are reasonable grounds to inquire into the matter, it may initiate an inquiry in respect thereof.

    (iii) **Sub Section 18** (3) states that the Central Information Commissioner, shall, while inquiring into any matter under this section, have the same powers as are vested in a civil court while trying a suit under the Code of Civil Procedure 1908, in respect of the matters listed in this sub section.

(b) **Section 19** lists out the procedure for filing an appeal and disposal thereof.

(c) **Section 20** lists out penalties under the Act.

Chapter VI

Chapter VI of the act gives out miscellaneous explanations and has following sections:-

(a) **Section 21** provides for protection of action taken in good faith.

(b) **Section 22** mention that the Act to have overriding effect on Official Secrets Act, 1923.

(c) **Section 23** bars courts from entertaining any suit, application or other proceeding in respect of any order made under this Act and no such order shall be called in question otherwise than by way of an appeal under this Act.

(d) **Section 24** lists out the organisations exempt from disclosure of information, less information pertaining to allegations of corruption and human rights violation, under the Act.

Important Definitions Covered in the RTI Act 2005.

Definitions. Some of the important definitions listed in the RTI Act 05 are reproduced below:-

(a) **"Appropriate Government"** means in relation to a public authority which is established, constituted, owned, controlled or substantially financed by funds provided directly or indirectly:-

    (i) By the Central Government or the Union territory administration, the Central Government.

    (ii) By the State Government, the State Government.

(b) **"Central Public Information Officer"** means the Central Public Information Officer designated under Sub-section (1) of Section 2 and including a Central Assistant Public Information Officer designated as such under sub-section (2) of section 5.

(c) **"Competent Authority" means:-**

    (i) The Speaker in the case of the House of the People or the Legislative Assembly of a State or a Union territory having such Assembly and the Chairman in the case of the Council of States or Legislative Council of a State.

    (ii) The Chief Justice of India in the case of the Supreme Court.

    (iii) The Chief Justice of the High Court in the case of a High Court.

(iv) The President or the Governor, as the case may be, in the case of other authorities established or constituted by or under the Constitution.

(v) The administrator appointed under Article 239 of the Constitution.

(d) **"Information"** means any material in any form, including records, documents, memos, e-mails, opinions, advices, press releases, circulars, orders, logbooks, contracts, reports, papers, samples, models, data material held in any electronic form and information relating to any private body which can be accessed by a public authority under any other law for the time being in force.

(e) **"Public Authority"** means any authority or body or institution of self- government established or constituted:-

(i) By or under the Constitution.

(ii) By any other law made by Parliament.

(iii) By any other law made by State Legislature.

(iv) By notification issued or order made by the appropriate Government and including any:-

(aa)   Body owned, controlled or substantially financed.

(ab)   Non-Government organisation substantially financed, di rectly or indirectly by funds provided by the appropriate Government.

(f) **"Record"** includes:-

(i) Any document, manuscript and file.

(ii) Any microfilm, microfiche and facsimile copy of a document.

(iii) Any reproduction of image or images embodied in such microfilm (whether enlarged or not).

(iv) Any other material produced by a computer or any other device.

(g) **"Right to Information"** means the right to information accessible under this Act which is held by or under the control of any public authority and including the right to:-

    (i) Inspection of work, documents, records.

    (ii) Taking notes extracts or certified copies of documents or records.

    (iii) Taking certified samples of material.

    (iv) Obtaining information in the form of diskettes, floppies, tapes, video cassettes or in any other electronic mode or through printouts where such information is stored in a computer or in any other device.

(h) **"Third Party"** means a person other than the citizen making a request for information and including a public authority.

Important Sections of RTI Act

Important sections which are repetitively referred to; are illustrated in succeeding paragraphs.

Obligations of Public Authorities.

Although obligations of public authorities are listed at Section 4 of the Act, certain important provisions are emphasized below:-

(a) **Section 4 (1).** Every public authority shall:-

    (i) **Section 4 (1) (a).** Maintain all its records duly catalogued and indexed in a manner and the form which facilitates the right to information under this Act and ensure that all records that are appropriate to be computerised, within a reasonable time. It is subjected to availability of resources, computerised and connected through a network all over the country on different systems so that access to such records is facilitated.

    (ii) **Section 4 (1)(b).** Publish within one hundred and twenty days from the enactment of this Act:

        (aa) The particulars of organisation, functions and duties.

(ab) The powers and duties of officers and employees.

(ac) The procedure followed in the decision making process, including channels of supervision and accountability.

(ad) The norms set for the discharge of its functions.

(ae) The rules, regulations, instructions, manuals and records, held or under control or used by employees for discharging functions.

(af) A directory consisting of details of officers and employees.

(ag) The monthly remuneration received by each of officers and employees, including the system of compensation as provided in regulations.

(ah) The budget allocated to each agency, indicating the particulars of all plans, proposed expenditures and reports on disbursements made.

(aj) The particulars of facilities available to citizens for obtaining information, including the working hours of a library or reading room, if maintained for public use.

(ak) The names, designations and other particulars of the Public Information Officers.

(al) Such other information as may be prescribed; and thereafter update these publications every year.

(iii) **Sec 4 (1)(d).** Provide reasons for its administrative or quasi-judicial decisions to affected persons.

(b) **Section 4 (2).** It shall be a constant endeavor of every public authority to take steps in accordance with the requirements of clause (b) of Sub-section (1) to provide as much information suo motu to the public at regular intervals, so that the public have minimum resort to the use of this Act to obtain information.

Duties of Central Public Information Officer/Public Information Officer.

Designation of Central Public Information Officer/Public Information Officer. Sub-section 5 (1) of the Act states that, every public authority shall designate as many officers as Central Public Information Officers/ Public Information Officers in all administrative units or offices under it as may be necessary to provide information to persons requesting information under this Act.

The duties of Central Public Information Officer/Public Information Officers, as given in the Act are as follows:-

(a) **Sub-section 5 (1).** Provide information to persons requesting information under this Act.

(b) **Sub-section 5 (2).** Receive the applications for information or appeals under this Act for forwarding the same forthwith to the Central Public Information Officer/ any other Public Information Officer or senior officer specified under Sub-section (1) of Section 19 (First Appellate Authority) or the Central Information Commission, as the case may be.

(c) **Sub-section 5 (3).** Render reasonable assistance to the persons seeking information.

(d) **Sub-section 6 (1).** Render all reasonable assistance to the person making the request orally to reduce the same in writing, where such request cannot be made in writing.

(e) **Sub-section 6 (2).** The Central Public Information Officer/Public Information Officer can not seek reasons for requesting information from the applicant.

(f) **Sub-section 6 (3).** Transfer the application or such part of it, as may be appropriate, to other Central Public Information Officer/ Public Information Officer with whom the information is held or to whose functions, the subject matter of information is more closely connected and information the applicant immediately about such transfer. The Central Public Information Officer/Public Information Officer will not return any application but will take action to transfer the same.

(g) **Sub-section 7 (1).** Provide the information or reject the request for any of the reasons specified in Sections 8 and 9, as expeditiously as possible.

(h) **Sub-section 7 (3).** Intimate applicant details of further fee (information material charges) representing the cost of providing the information, together with the calculations made to arrive at the amount and also information the applicant about his or her right to appeal against the fee charged or the form of access provided, including the particulars of the appellate authority and time limit.

(j) **Sub-section 7 (4).** Provide assistance to enable access to the information, including providing such assistance as may be appropriate for the inspection, where access to information is required to be provided to a person who is sensory disabled.

(k) **Sub-section 7 (7).** Take into consideration the representation made by a third party under section 11, before taking any decision under Sub-section 7(1).

(l) **Sub-section 7 (8).** Communicate the following while rejecting a request under Sub-section 7(1):-

(i) The reasons for such rejection (quoting the exact section of the Act).

(ii) The period within which an appeal against such rejection may be preferred.

(iii) The particulars of the appellate authority.

(m) **Sub-section 7 (9).** This states that information shall ordinarily be provided in the form in which it is sought unless it would disproportionately divert the resources of the public authority or would be detrimental to the safety or preservation of the record in question. This implies that although the Act makes it obligatory for the public authorities to maintain information in the form that facilitates right to information however, if the information is not available in the form it has been sought and doing so would disproportionately divert the resources of the public authority, then information would be provided as available and the Central Public Information Officer/Public Information Officer is not obliged to collate the same (CIC Decision No 392/IC (A)/2006 dated 28 Nov 06 in the case of RSS Kumari Vs HPCL refers).

Exemptions.

It is pertinent to highlight that under the Act, right to information is the rule and exemptions therein are exceptions, implying that these exemptions should not be exercised arbitrarily by the public authorities to deny citizens their right to information. The exemptions should be used exceptionally and judiciously, for denying information. The disclosure of which would cause greater harm than the public interest served in disclosing such information.

Exemptions under Section 8.

(a) **Sub-section 8 (1)** states that notwithstanding anything contained in this Act, there shall be no obligation on public authority to provision information to any citizen:-

(i) **8 (1) (a).** Information, disclosure of which would prejudicially affect the sovereignty and integrity of India, the security, strategic, scientific or economic interests of the State, relation with foreign State or lead to incitement of an offence.

(ii) **8 (1)(b).** Information which has been expressly forbidden to be published by any court of law or tribunal or the disclosure of which may constitute contempt of court. This is also an enabling provision as this implies that information can not be denied just because the case is sub-judice in a court of law (CIC Decision No CIC/AT/A/2006/00126 dated 14 Jul 06 in the case of Shri Keshav Kumar Bhardwaj Vs NCRB refers).

(iii) **8 (1)(c).** Information, the disclosure of which would cause a breach of privilege of Parliament or the State Legislature.

(iv) **8 (1)(d).** Information including commercial confidence, trade secrets or intellectual property, the disclosure of which would harm the competitive position of a third party, unless the competent authority is satisfied that larger public interest warrants the disclosure of such information.

(v) **8 (1)(e).** Information available to a person in his fiduciary relationship, unless the competent authority is satisfied that the larger public interest warrants the disclosure of such information.

(vi) **8 (1)(f).** Information received in confidence from foreign Government.

(vii) **8 (1)(g).** Information, the disclosure of which would endanger the life or physical safety of any person or identify the source of information or assistance given in confidence for law enforcement or security purposes.

(viii) **8 (1)(h).** Information which would impede the process of investigation or apprehension or prosecution of offenders.

(ix) **8 (1)(i).** Cabinet papers including records of deliberations of the Council of Ministers, Secretaries and other officers; provided that the decisions of Council of Ministers, the reasons thereof, and the material on the basis of which the decisions were taken shall be made public after the decision has been taken, and the matter is complete, or over; provided further that those matters which come under the exemptions specified in this section shall not be disclosed.

(x) **8 (1)(j).** Information which relates to personal information the disclosure of which has no relationship to any public activity or interest, or which would cause unwarranted invasion of the privacy of the individual unless the Central Public Information Officer or the State Public Information Officer or the appellate authority, as the case may be, is satisfied that the larger public interest justifies the disclosure of such information; it may be noted that the information which cannot be denied to the Parliament or a State Legislature shall not be denied to any person.

(b) **Sub-section 8 (2)** states that notwithstanding anything in the Official Secrets Act, 1923 nor any of the exemptions permissible in accordance with sub-section (1), a public authority may allow access to information, if public interest in disclosure outweighs the harm to the protected interests.

(c) **Sub-section 8 (3)** states that, subject to the provisions of clauses (a), (c) and (i) of sub-section (1), any information relating to any occurrence, event or matter which has taken place, occurred or happened twenty years before the date on which any request is made under Section 6, shall be provided. However, maintenance and weeding of records will be carried out as per rules and regulations applicable in the organization and as directed by DoPT from time to time.

Exemptions under Section 9.

It states that without prejudice to the provisions of Section 8, the CPIO/PIO, may reject a request for information where such a request for providing access would involve an infringement of copyright subsisting in a person other than the State.

Section 10 - Severability Clause.

Sub-section 10. In case of information exempt under the Act, this section provides for access to that part of the record which does not contain any information which is exempt from disclosure under this Act and which can reasonably be severed from any part that contains exempt information. Where access is granted to a part of the record , the Central Public Information Officer/Public Information Officer shall give a notice to the applicant, information that only part of the record requested, after severance of the record containing information which is exempt from disclosure, is being provided; the reasons for the decision, including any findings on any material question of fact, referring to the material on which those findings were based; the name and designation of the person giving the decision; the details of the fees calculated and the amount of fee which is required to deposited; and rights of the applicant with respect to review of the decision regarding non-disclosure of part of the information, the amount of fee charged or the form of access provided, including the particulars of the first Appellate Authority, time limit, process and any other form of access.

Section 11- Third Party Information.

Where Central Public Information Officer/Public Information Officer intends to disclose any information or record, which relates to a third party and has been treated as confidential by that third party, he/she shall, within five days from the receipt of the request, give a written notice to third party of such request and of the fact that he/she, intends to disclose the information, and invite the third party to make a submission in writing or orally, whether the information should be disclosed or otherwise. And such submission of the third party shall be kept in view while taking a decision about disclosure of information. It may not be provided in the case of trade or commercial secrets protected by law, disclosure may be allowed if the public interest outweighs in importance any possible harm or injury to the interests of such third party. The Central Public Information Officer/Public Information Officer shall make a decision whether or not to disclose the information and give in writing the notice of his decision to the third party. A notice given under Sub-section (3) shall include a statement that the third party to whom the notice is given is entitled to prefer an appeal under Section 19 against the decision.

Section 12– 14 Central Information Commission.

Section 12 to 14 of the Act deals with constitution of the Central information Commission (hereafter referred as CIC), its term of office, condition and removal. The Central Government shall by notification in the Official Gazette, constitute a body to be known as Central Information Commission to exercise the powers conferred on, and to perform the function assigned to, it under this Act.

Section 15– 17 State Information Commission.

Section 15 to 18 of the Act deals with constitution of the State information Commission, its term of office, condition and removal. Every State Government shall by notification in the Official Gazette, constitute a body to be known as (Name of the state) State Information Commission e.g. Haryana State Information Commission to exercise the powers conferred on, and to perform the function assigned to, it under this Act.

Since the scope of this paper confined to implications of RTI Act 05 to the Armed Forces which is a public authority under Central Government, the State Information Commission is not discussed in detail hereafter; however nature of functions of the State Information Commission and statutory provisions while discharging the duties is similar to that of the CIC.

Section 18-20 Power and Function of information Commissions.

Detailed guidelines on power, function, appeal and penalties are covered in section 18 to 20 of the said Act. The provisions of these guidelines are enumerated in succeeding paragraphs.

Section 21 – Protection of action taken in Good Faith.

No suit, prosecution or other legal proceeding shall lie against any person for anything which in good faith done or intended to be done under this Act or any rule made there under.

Section 22 – Act to have Overriding Effect.

The provisions of RTI Act shall have effect not withstanding anything inconsistent therewith contained in the Official Secret Act, 1923 and any other law for the time being in force or in any instrument having effect by virtue of any law other than this Act. This defines that no law of the land can prevent to disclose information by the CPIO in case if it serves larger public interest.

Section – 23 Bar of Jurisdiction of Courts.

No court of the country shall entertain any suit, application or other proceedings in respect of any order made under this Act and no such order shall be called in question otherwise than by way of appeal under this Act. Such provision does help information holder and seeker to amicably settle issues raised trough appeal and prevent misuse of judicial machinery.

Section – 24 Act not to apply to Certain Organization.

Certain Intelligence and security organisations which have been specified in the second schedule have been kept out of the purview of RTI Act 05, however if information pertaining to the allegations of corruption and human rights violations shall not be excluded. Further it has also been amplified that if information sought for pertains to violation of human rights, information shall only be provided after the approval of the Central Information Commissioner and notwithstanding anything contained in section 7 of the Act. There are a total 22 Intelligence and Security Organisations established by the Central Government and are included in the second schedule of the Act. The details of these organisation is as under:-

(a) Intelligence Bureau.

(b) Research and Analysis wing of Cabinet Secretariat.

(c) Directorate of Revenue Intelligence.

(d) Central Economic Intelligence Bureau.

(e) Directorate of Enforcement.

(f) Narcotics Control Bureau.

(g) Aviation Research Centre.

(h) Special Frontier Force.

(j) Border Security Force.

(k) Central Reserve Police Force.

(l) Indo-Tibet Border Police.

(m) Central Industrial Security Force.

(n) National Security Guards.

(o) Assam Rifles.

(p) Sashatra Seema Bal.

(q) Directorate General of Income Tax (Investigation)

(r) National Technical Research organization.

(s) Financial Intelligence Unit, India.

(t) Special Protection Group.

(v) Defence Research and Development Organisation.

(w) Border Road Development Board.

(x) National Security Council Secretariat

Section – 25 Monitoring and Reporting

This section specifies annual report on implementation of the provision of the Act to be prepared by the Central and State Information Commission every year and submit it to the appropriate Government. The annual report is to be prepared by all public authorities containing number of requests made, number of appeals, denial of information, disciplinary action if any, amount collected, any facts indicate efforts of Public Authority in the spirit of the act and recommendations if any for reform etc are to be covered in detail.

Section - 26 to 30 Role of Government.

Section 26, 27, 28, 29 & 30 of the Act gives out the role of the appropriate Government in preparing training programmes, framing rules regarding fee, salary and allowances, laying of rules and power to remove difficulties in giving effect to the provisions of this Act.

Chapter 3
Appeals and its Methodology

Appeal

An information seeker may prefer appeal as per section 19 of the Act, in case information not received in stipulated time or aggrieved with the information provisioned to him. Initially appeal is made to the officer senior in rank to the Central Public Information Officer known as First Appeal. Later Second Appeal against the decision shall lie with in 90 days to the Central Information Commission. Some of the common causes of preferring appeal are as under:-

(a) Refusal to Accept Application

(b) Information Not Provided

(c) Information Not Provided Within Stipulated Period

(d) Incorrect Information

(e) Incomplete Information

(f) Wrong Denial

(g) Wrong Fee Asked

New Inputs during Appeal. The appellant cannot raise request for fresh items of information in his/her appeal. Appeal can be preferred only with respect to information sought in the original application. CIC decision No

CIC/AT/A/2006/00128 dated 13 Jul 06, in the case of Shri AH Sahore Vs Coast Guards, refers.

First Appeal

Appeal to First Appellate Authority Any person who, does not receive a decision within the time specified in sub-section (1) or clause (a) of sub-section (3) of section 7, or is aggrieved by a decision of the Central Public Information Officer/Public Information Officer as the case may be, may within thirty days from the expiry of such period or from the receipt of such a decision prefer an appeal to first Appellate Authority. First Appellate Authority may admit an appeal after the expiry of the period of thirty days if he or she is satisfied that the appellant was prevented by sufficient cause from filing the appeal in time (Sub-section 19(1) refers).

Duties of Appellate Authority. The first Appellate Authority is an officer superior to the Central Public Information Officer/Public Information Officer, as the case may be, and is designated under the provisions of Sub- section 19 (1) of the Act. Being an officer senior to the CPIO/PIO, it is the responsibility of the first Appellate authority to receive appeals under Section 19 of the Act and take necessary action to dispose them as expeditiously as possible, but not later than the time period specified under the Act. There are numerous policy letters issued by the Department of Personnel & Training, Government of India vide their Memorandum No 1/3/2008-IR.

Deciding appeals under the Act is a quasi-judicial function and it is, therefore, necessary that the Appellate Authority should see to it that justice is not only done but it should also appear to have been done. In order to do so, the order passed by the appellate authority should be a speaking order giving justification for the decision arrived at. In this context a detailed Office Memorandum No 10/23/2007-IR dated 09 Jul 07 has been issued by the DOPT as guidelines for Disposal of Appeals under RTI Act 05 which can be referred to.

Disposal of appeal by first Appellate Authority. An appeal under Sub-section 19(1) or Sub-section 19(2) shall be disposed of within thirty days of the receipt of the appeal or within such extended period not exceeding a total of forty-five days from the date of filing thereof, as the case may be, for reasons to be recorded in writing (Sub-section 19(6) refers).

Methodology of handling First Appeal. On receipt of the first appeal a brief of the case is forwarded to the Appellate Authority. The case file will be prepared for the hearing. A copy of the appeal is forwarded to all the concerned departments /offices whose assistance was sought in providing information to the applicant. Thereafter, the first Appellate Authority may call for hearing on the case. The CPIO/PIO and representatives of the concerned office/department should generally attend the hearing. The Appellate Authority shall go through the contents of the appeal and give his decision in the form of a speaking order as stated in preceding paragraphs. Once decision has been given by the Appellate Authority, the Public Information Officer shall initiate action to provide further information or dispose off the appeal, as the case may be, in accordance with the decision by the First Appellate Authority. The onus to prove that a denial of a request was justified shall be on the CPIO/PIO, who denied the request, under the provisions of Sub-section 19 (5) of the Act.

Second Appeal

A second appeal against the decision under sub-section (1) shall lie, with the Central Information Commission (hereafter referred at times as CIC), under the provisions of Sub- section 19 (3) of the Act. CIC (Appeal Procedure) Rules, 2005 is also elaborated by Department of Personnel and Training (DOP&T) Government of India vide its Notification No 1/4/2005-IR dated 28 Oct 05.

Central Information Commission.

Central Information Commission is constituted by the Central Government through a Gazette Notification. The Commission including one Chief Information Commissioner (CIC) and not more than 10 Information Commissioners (IC); are appointed by the President of India. The Central Information Commission/State Information Commission has a duty to receive complaint/second appeal from any person:-

(a) Who has not been able to submit an information request because a Public Information Officer has not been appointed.

(b) Who has been refused information that was requested.

(c) Who has received no response to his/her information request within the specified time limits.

(d) Who thinks the fees charged are unreasonable.

(e) Who thinks the fees charged are unreasonable.

(f) Who thinks information given is incomplete or false or misleading.

(g) Any other matter relating to obtaining information under this law.

Central Information Commission has power to order inquiry if there are reasonable grounds. Central Information Commissioner/State Information Commissioner as the case may have powers of Civil Court such as:-

(a) Summoning and enforcing attendance of persons, compelling them to give oral or written evidence on oath and to produce documents or things.

(b) Requiring the discovery and inspection of documents.

(c) Receiving evidence on affidavit.

(d) Requisitioning public records or copies from any court or office.

(e) Issuing summons for examination of witnesses or documents.

(f) Any other matter which may be prescribed.

All records covered by this law (including those covered by exemptions) are given to Central Information Commissioner/State Information Commissioner during inquiry for examination. Power to secure compliance of its decisions from the Public Authority including:-

(a) Providing access to information in a particular form.

(b) Directing the public authority to appoint a Public Information Officer/Assistant Public Information Officer where none exists.

(c) Publishing information or categories of information.

(d) Making necessary changes to the practices relating to management, maintenance and destruction of records.

(e) Enhancing training provision for officials on RTI.

(f) Seeking an annual report from the public authority on compliance with   this   law.

(g) Require it to compensate for any loss or other detriment suffered by the   applicant.

(h) Impose penalties under this law.

(j) Reject the application.

Procedure for Deciding Appeal by Central Information Commission.

In deciding appeal, the commission may

(a) Hear oral or written evidence on oath or an affidavit concerned or interested person;

(b) Peruse or inspect documents, public records or copies thereof;

(c) Inquire through authorized officer further details or facts;

(d) Hear Central Public Information Officer or such senior officer who decided the first appeal, or such person against whom the complaint is made, as the case may be;

(e) Hear third party; and

(f) Receive evidence on affidavits from Central Public Information Officer, such senior officer who decided the first appeal, or such person against whom the complaint lies or the third party.

Penalties

Where the Central Information Commissioner is of the opinion that the CPIO/PIO, without any reasonable cause, refused to receive an application for information or has not furnished information within the time specified under Sub-section (1) of Section 7 or intentionally denied the request for information or knowingly given incorrect, incomplete or misleading information or destroyed information which was the subject of the request or obstructed in any manner in furnishing the information, it shall impose a penalty of two hundred and fifty rupees each day till application is received or information is furnished, so however, the total amount of such penalty shall not exceed twenty-five thousand rupees (Sub-section 20(1) refers).

Where the Central Information Commission is of the opinion that the Chief Public Information Officer/Public Information Officer, has, without any reasonable cause and persistently, failed to receive an application for information or has not furnished information within the time specified under Sub-section (1) of Section 7 or malafidely denied the request for information or knowingly given incorrect, incomplete or misleading information or destroyed information which was the subject of the request or obstructed in any manner in furnishing the information, it shall recommend for disciplinary action against the Central Public Information Officer/Public Information Officer, under the service rules applicable to him/her (Sub-section 20(2) refers).

Timeline

Timeline for various actions under the Act is given in succeeding paragraphs.

(a) 30 days from receipt of application under normal circumstances (Sub-section 7(1) refers).

(b) 48 hours of receipt of the request, where the information sought for concerns the life or liberty of a person (Sub-section 7(1) refers).

(c) Where further fees representing the cost of providing the information has been sought from the applicant, the period intervening between the dispatch of the said intimation and payment of fees shall be excluded for the purpose of calculating the period of thirty days (Sub-subsection 7(3)(a) refers).

(d) Where an application for information or appeal is given to a Central Assistant Public Information Officer (a different PUBLIC INFORMATION OFFICER, other than who has provided the information, in the case of the Indian army) a period of five days (total 35 days) shall be added in computing the period for response specified under Sub-section (1) of Section 7 (Sub-section 5(2) refers).

(e) Where information is sought from intelligence and security organizations, in respect of allegations of violation of human rights, the information shall only be provided after the approval of the Central Information Commission, and notwithstanding anything contained in Section 7, such information shall be provided within 45 days from the date of the receipt of request.

Notice to Third Party Where the Central Public Information Officer/ Public Information Officer intends to disclose any information, which relates to or has been supplied by a third party he/she shall, within five days from the receipt of the request, give a written notice to such third party of the request and of the fact that he/she intends to disclose the information and invite the third party to make a submission in writing or orally, regarding whether the information should be disclosed (Sub-section 11(1) refers).

Reply to Notice by Third Party Where a notice is served by the CPIO/ PIO under Sub-section 11 (1) to a third party in respect of any information, the third party shall, within ten days from the date of receipt of such notice, be given the opportunity to make representation against the proposed disclosure (Sub-section 11(2) refers).

Information not Held on Record The Central Public Information Officer/ Public Information Officer can provide information that is available on records and in material form. There is no obligation on him/her to create or collate information. If the information is not available he can information the applicant about the same. (CIC Decision on Appeal No 1343/ICPB/2008 dated 22 Jan 08, in the case of Professor SP Singh Vs Nehru Memorial Museum & Library refers)

Sensitive Personal Data At times citizen seek information under the Act which can be categorized as sensitive personnel facts and can be denied to applicant under RTI Act. Though not appropriately classified, however based on a decision of the CIC, following is termed as sensitive personnel data which cane be referred to in case required:- (CIC decision WB /B/A/2007/00420 date 11 Apr 2007 refers)

- The racial or ethnic origin of the data subject.

- His political opinions.

- His religious beliefs or other beliefs of a similar nature.

- Whether he is a member of a trade union.

- His physical or mental health or condition.

- His sexual life.

- The commission or alleged commission by him of any offence.

- Any proceedings for any offence committed or alleged to have been committed by him, the disposal of such proceedings or the sentence of any court in such proceedings.

Use of Hindi Language (Rajbhasha) With a view to propagate use of official language Hindi in Central Government Organisations and to facilitate citizen for better comprehension of response received under RTI Act from CPIO, recently Ministry of Home Affairs has issued out a policy applicable to all Central Organisations that applications received written in Hindi language from citizen seeking information under RTI Act to respond in HINDI language only. This may put extra burden on Armed Forces as most of the Correspondence is held in English language and not much infrastructure exist at all offices in terms of translators etc.

Chapter 4
Implementation of RTI Act in Armed Forces

With the increase in awareness amongst the pubic, the RTI mechanism amongst the public authorities is envisage to tackle major challenges to meet the aspiration of citizens. There are few public authorities who have already realised this fact and initiated necessary measures to increase transparency in their functioning and satiate the citizens' quest for information. Armed Forces after initial resistance have swung into action in the year 2007 and set up efficient mechanism at various levels to meet the requirements. Implementation of RTI Act 2005 in the Armed Forces is covered separately for three services in subsequent paragraphs.

Indian Army

Since Indian Army is a public authority and also covered under the provisions of this Act and therefore there is requirement to fulfill its obligation under sec 4 of RTI Act, accordingly, in the year 2007, a formal raising of the RTI Cell was ordered and an RTI Cell was established under Additional Director General Public Information at Army Headquarters. The time frame of hundred days for implementation of the Act necessitated immediate steps to be taken to appoint Central Public Information Officers (CPIO)/Public Information Officers (PIO) and First Appellate Authorities (FAA) within the public authorities. Unlike a conventional new raising, which is done after considerable planning and forethought, the raising of RTI Cell and an organisation for its implementation in the Army had to be completed in a very short time of 100 days and hence giving the RTI Organisation a final shape has been a dynamic process incorporating major changes as knowledge about the Act and its implications grew. As awareness about the RTI Act 05 grew, it was envisaged that the requests for information would increase manifold. Keeping this in mind, Public Information Officers (Public Information Officers) and Appellate Authorities (AA) at all subordinate formation Headquarters were notified and promulgated.

During the year 2008, based on recommendations by Perspective Planning Directorate, then Chief of The Army Staff entrusted responsibility to administer RTI Act in the Army to Army Educational Corps. Since then, Additional Director General Army education (ADGAE) is overall responsible to administer RTI and its related issues. Thus most of the officers handling RTI mechanism are from the Army Education Corps and have been employed as Public Information Officers (PIOs) at various levels. Also Directorate of Staff Duties at Army Headquarters had promulgated detailed instructions covering aspects like level, type, charter, appointment of officials etc for smooth implementation of the RTI Act with in the Indian Army.

RTI Cell – Nodal Agency. RTI Cell established at Army Headquarters has been made as a nodal agency for implementation and smooth functioning of RTI mechanism and monitor activities undertaken by PIOS of subordinate formation Headquarters of the Army. Since then there have been numerous policy letters issued by the RTI Cell and number of training session cum workshops have been conducted at various locations with a view to train Public Information Officers and educate environment on nuances of the said Act.

RTI Organisation in the Army.

At Army Headquarters. With a view to be fair with the appellant seeking information and to augment accountability, the FAA and PIO in the Army have been deputed to be from two different branches of the Army i.e. FAA is from A branch whereas PIO is from G branch. Accordingly at Army Headquarters, the duties of First Appellate Authority is discharged by a Maj Gen rank officer from AG's branch as of now, Provost Marshal is the FAA and CPIO is a Brig rank officer posted at Military Training

Directorate, GS branch as DDGMTI(RTI/AEC) who heads the RTI Cell. The organization of RTI Cell at Integrated Headquarters of Ministry of Defence (Army) is as under:-

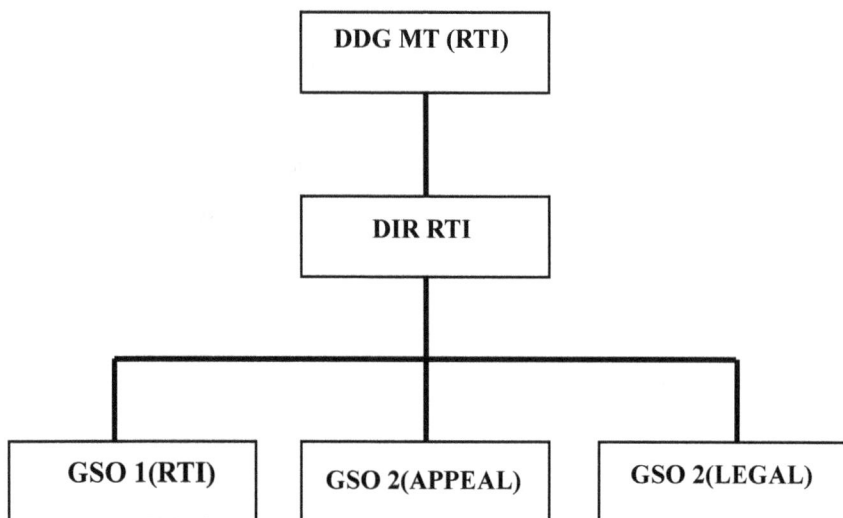

```
              ┌──────────────────┐
              │   DDG MT (RTI)   │
              └────────┬─────────┘
                       │
              ┌────────┴─────────┐
              │     DIR RTI      │
              └────────┬─────────┘
          ┌────────────┼────────────┐
┌─────────────┐ ┌──────────────┐ ┌──────────────┐
│  GSO 1(RTI) │ │GSO 2(APPEAL) │ │ GSO 2(LEGAL) │
└─────────────┘ └──────────────┘ └──────────────┘
```

FIRST APPELLATE AUTHORITY – PROVOST MARSHAL

At Subordinate Formations In the Army, the designation of Public Information Officers has however, been done down to the formation level only, as it is considered essential that information provided under the Act should be adequately vetted and delegating the same down to unit level may lead to breach of security as also hinder their operational functioning. For details of Central Public Information Officer/Public Information Officer and Appellate authorities in the Army, Staff Duties Directorate of Integrated Headquarters of Ministry of Defence have issued Comprehensive Instructions vide their Letter No A/30201/1/SD-8 dated 15 Jul 08 and A/30201/1/SD-8 dated 19 Jan 11, respectively. The RTI org at subordinate formations of the Army is as under:-

FORMATION/ ESTABLISHMENT	PUBLIC INFORMATION OFFICER	FIRST APPELLATTE AUTHORITY
HEADQUARTERS COMDS (LESS ARTRAC)	BRIG/COL (EDN)	COS/BRIG ADM
HEADQUARTERS ARTRAC	COL A	BRIG ADM
CORPS HEADQUARTERS	COL (EDN)/SO 1(EDN)	BRIG A/BRIG ADM
DIV HEADQUARTERS	SO 1/SO 2 (EDN)	DY GOC
BDE HEADQUARTERS	EDN OFFR	DY CDR
AREA HEADQUARTERS	COL GS/SO 1 (EDN)	DY GOC/BRIG ADM
SUB AREA HEADQUARTERS	COL GS/SO 1 (EDN)	STATION COMMANDER
CAT A ESTABLISHMENT	COL GS/SO 1 (EDN)	DY COMDT/CHIEF INSTRUCTOR
CAT B ESTABILSHMENT	COL GS/SO 1(EDN)	DY COMDT/CHIEF INSTRUCTOR
REGIMENTAL CENTRES	COL GS/SO 1(EDN)	DY COMDT
RECORDS OFFICES	CRO/SRO	DY COMDT OF REGTL CENTRE
ARMY BASE WORKSHOP/ADVANCE BASE WORKSHOP	2IC/ADM OFFR	COMMANDANT
ORDANANCE DEPOTs		
(CODs/CVDs)	ADM OFFR	COMMANDANT
HOSPITALS		
(CH/BH/MH)	BRIG I/C ADM/SR REGISTRAR & OC TPS/ REGISTRAR	COMMANDANT
HEADQUARTERS RTG ZONES	DIR RTG (STATES)	DDG RTG (STATES)
IRO	DY IRO (B) OR OFFR OFFG	DIR RTG
RIMC/RASHTRIYA MIL SCHOOLS	ADM OFFR	PRINCIPAL

Update on Army Intranet.   In consonance with the sec 4(b) of the RTI Act 2005 and with a view to keep environment informed on the RTI activities, a RTI link on the Army Intranet is hosted on the home page. The information hosted on the NET helps in increasing awareness amongst the troops about the Act i.e. what information is available and what is not open to disclosure to avoid inconsequential applications. It also to assist the Public Information Officers entrusted with the task of providing information under the Act.   A hyper link on the home page is leading to the RTI main page, which essentially, constitutes of the following:-

(a)   RTI Act.

(b)   Summary of Sec & Sub Sec of RTI Act.

(c)   RTI org.

(d)   Procedure for seeking information.

(e)   Procedure for First Appeal.

(f)   What is exempted from disclosure?

(g)   Guidelines for PIO.

(h)   Defending of RTI cases at CIC.

(j)   Imp CIC decisions.

(k)   FAQs.

Update of Status of Case on Internet Also, with a view to facilitate appellant to know his status of application e.g. application received, case number allotted and progress thereof, a module has been incorporated into website of Indian Army on the Internet (indianarmy.nic.in) which facilitate appellant to view progress of the case once case number is entered.

Indian Navy

In accordance with the guidelines issued by the Ministry of Defence, Indian Navy also set up their RTI organization at Headquarters and at all of its subordinate formations in the year 2006. The responsibility of administrating RTI cases is with the officers posted at Personnel and Administration branch of the Indian Navy. A director level officer of the rank of Captain is the CPIO and a duty of FAA is performed by on officer of the rank of Vice Admiral, Chief of Personnel Services. Public Information Officers are deputed at each Command Headquarters and few Assistant Public Information Officer (APIO) are also deputed at outlying units.   The workload and trends of cases of Indian Navy is discussed in the next chapter.

Indian Air Force

The responsibility of administrating RTI cases in Indian Air Force lies with the Administrative or legal branch. In consonance with the RTI framework, At Air Force Headquarter, the RTI set up functions at Vayu Bhawan, under the aegis of Directorate of Personnel Services wherein a Director level officer of the rank of Group Captain act as a CPIO and a Joint Director level officer assist him. The Duties of First Appellate Authority is performed by Air Officer in charge Administration (AOA). Also CPIOs are appointed at every Command Headquarters and few APIOs are deputed at selected station.

Chapter 5
Trends of RTI Cases in the Armed Forces

Trends of cases received at the RTI cells of Integrated Headquarters of Ministry of Defence consisting of Army, Navy and Air Force are enumerated at successive paragraphs.

Indian Army

Workload at the RTI Cell

Summary of RTI applications/ appeals received at the RTI Cell of Army Headquarters till 31 Dec 2012 since inception is as under:-

    (a) RTI applications recd   -   16471

    (b) No of case processed with Branches/Directorate -   10948

    (c) No of cases transferred to other PIOs   -   4632

    (d) Applications technically invalid/Rejected   -   891

    (e) 1st Appeals disposed off   -   2250

    (f) 2nd Appeals disposed off   -   424

As awareness of RTI is rapidly growing in our country, demand from citizen seeking information under the Act is growing exponentially. Year wise details of cases are given below. The increasing trend is evident from the graph shown under:-

Fig 1

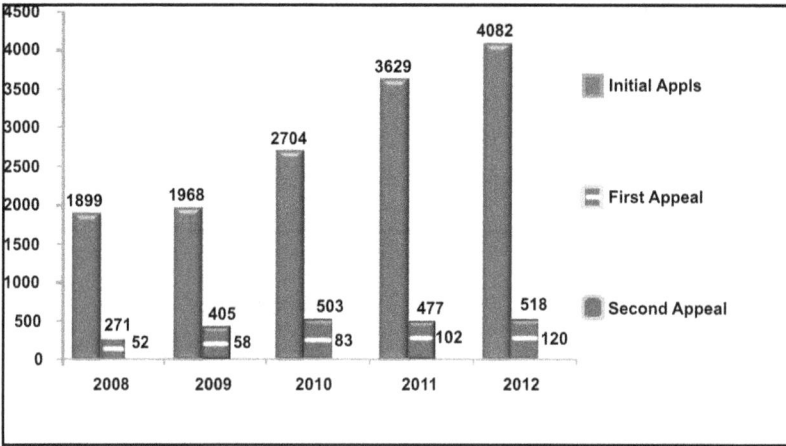

Year wise workload of RTI cases at Army Headquarters

The information sought is on diversified subjects, however maximum number of issues on which information is sought pertains to A matters held with the Adjutant General's Branch followed by Military Secretary Branch. The graphical analysis is illustrated below. For ease of sampling the trend, a total of 6531 cases have been taken into account.

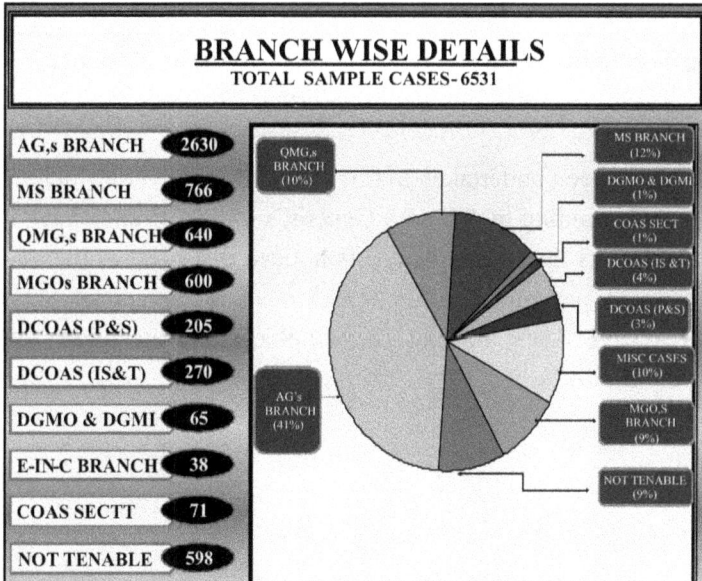

BRANCH WISE DETAILS
TOTAL SAMPLE CASES- 6531

AG,s BRANCH	2630
MS BRANCH	766
QMG,s BRANCH	640
MGOs BRANCH	600
DCOAS (P&S)	205
DCOAS (IS&T)	270
DGMO & DGMI	65
E-IN-C BRANCH	38
COAS SECTT	71
NOT TENABLE	598

Fig 2 : Branch wise trend of RTI Cases

It is also observed that besides large number of citizens requesting for information under the said act, serving and retired officers of the armed forces also resort to RTI act for either resolving their own problems or seeking generic nature of information. Out of 6531 sample cases, almost 2500 cases have been filed by only officers of Armed forces including serving and retired. The graphical analysis is given out as under:-

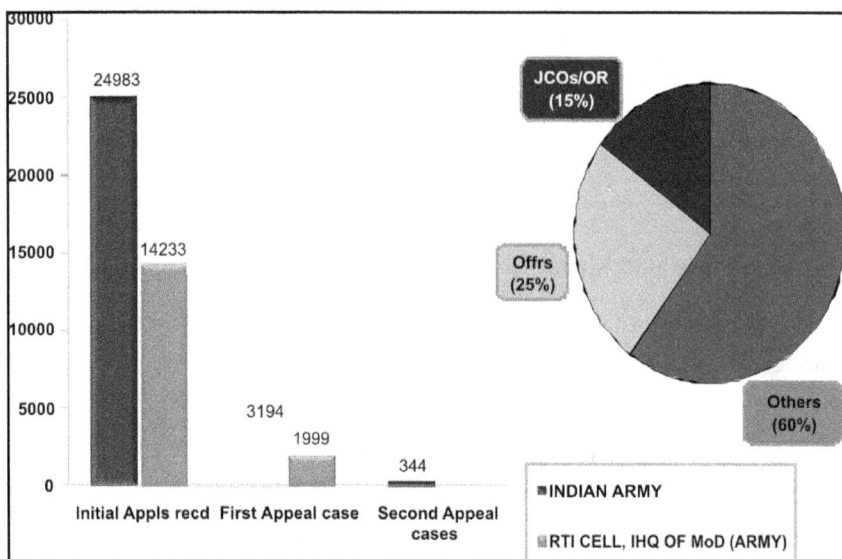

Fig 3 : Number of cases received in the Army as on 30 Jun 12

Attempt has also been undertaken to find out cases related to which major areas/subjects pertaining to Adjutant General's (AG's) Branch have been asked by applicants time and again. It is noticed that most of the queries sought relates to pay and pension issues dealt by Personnel Services Directorate of the AG's branch. The graphical analysis given below elucidates the details.

TRENDS AT AG's BRANCH

(Ags BRANCH - SAMPLE CASES –2630)

PAY, ALLCES & PENSION	1063
RULES & POLICIES	153
DISCIPLINE	326
RECRUTING	139
STAT/NON STAT COMPLAINTS	198
ECHS	186
MED FACILITIES	249
HONOURS & AWARDS	86
MISC	230

RECRUITMENTS (5%)
DISCIPLINE (12%)
STAT/ NON STAT COMPLAINTS (8%)
ECHS (7%)
PAY, ALLC E & PENSION (41%)
MED FACILITIES (9%)
HONOURS & AWARDS (3%)
RULES & POLICIES (6%)
MISC (9%)

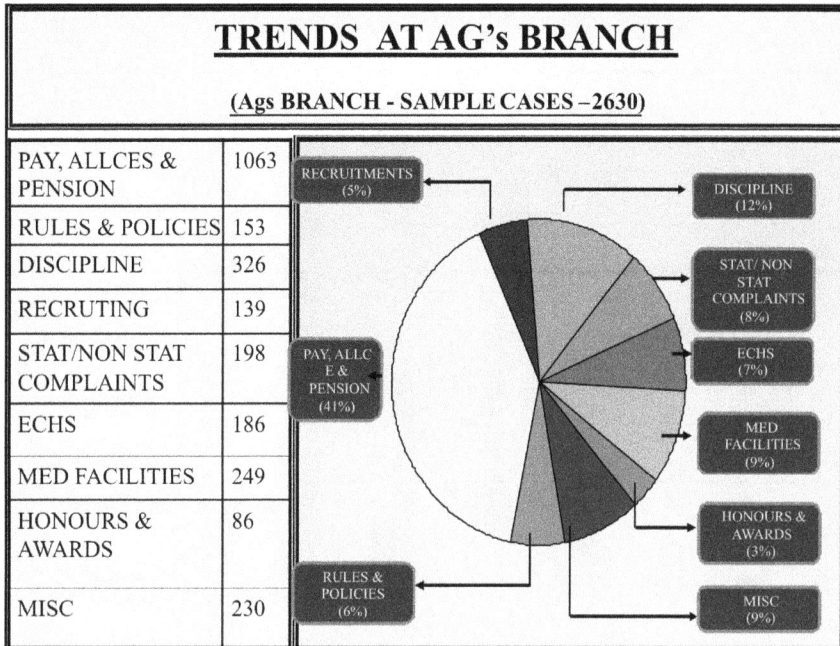

Fig 4 : Trends of RTI Cases at AG's Branch of the Army

Indian Navy

As awareness grew, the quantum of RTI cases in the Indian Navy also started swelling. The year wise breakdown of cases is as follows:-

Year	Applications received	Appeal to FAA	Appeal to CIC
2007	161	42	08
2008	239	74	12
2009	343	109	33
2010	450	110	15
2011	441	115	23
2012	717	83	18

The graphical picture given below clearly indicates increasing trends of RTI cases at Headquarters of Indian Navy.

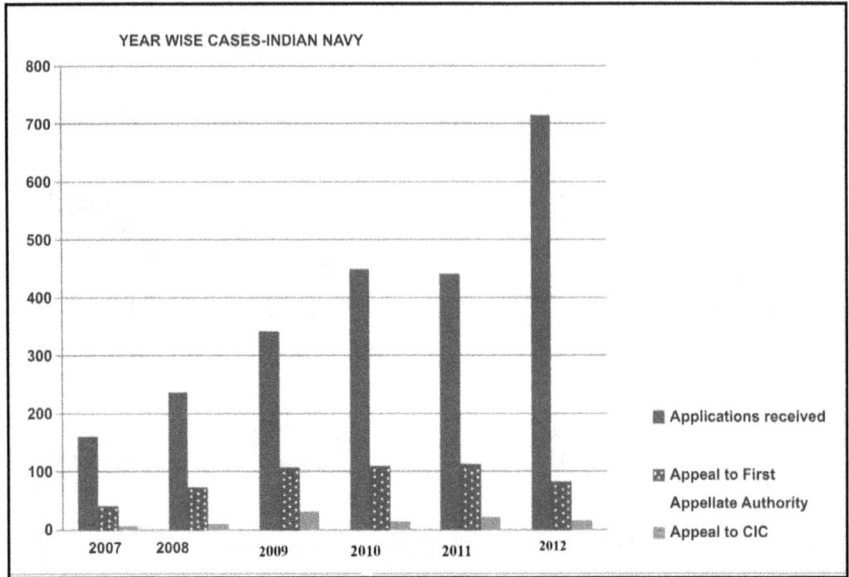

Fig 5 : Year wise work Load RTI Cases- Indian Navy

Theme of the Information Sought at Naval HQ Generally information sought is related to personnel issues. Major subjects on whom frequently information is sought are as under:-

(a) Status of Premature Retirement

(b) Status of Representation filed

(c) Documents related to Trials and Inquiries

(d) Status of Pensioner Claims and Retirement Benefits

(e) Documents relating to Medical Re-Classification

Indian Air Force

Trends of Cases

The year wise workload of RTI cases at the Air Headquarters is as under:-

Year	Initial Application	First Appeal	Second Appeal
2006	124	31	11
2007	250	56	05
2008	247	56	08
2009	557	99	33
2010	1182	155	23
2011	1555	198	23
2012	1539	212	23

Graphical representation of the work load at RTI Cell of Air Headquarters is under:-

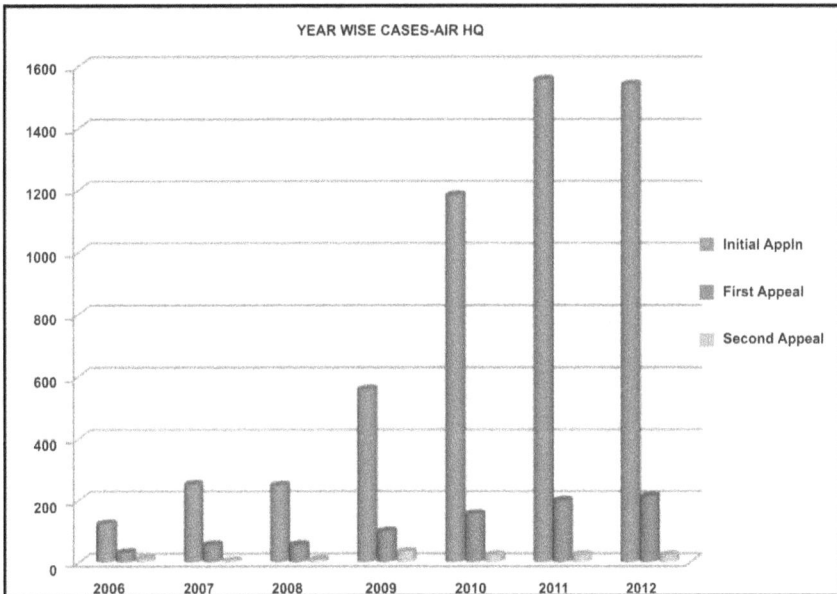

Fig : 6 Year wise workload at the Air Force Headquarters

Theme of the Information Sought   Major subjects for which information is sought repetitively by citizens from CPIO of Air Force are as follows:-

(a) Personnel Issues like Pay fixation, Pension, Retirement benefits

(b) Airlift to VIPs

(c) Examination for recruitment

(d) Details of aircraft accident and financial loss suffered

(e)   Copies of Medical Examinations

(f) Details of works undertaken

Common Trends

Officers Dominance Large number of information seekers is either serving or retired officers of the Armed Forces. Most of the issues raised are close to their own personal issues which are pending at various directorates of the Armed Forces. The RTI route undertaken is to build pressure on officials to deal with their cases expeditiously. This approach in any case does not achieve the aim of RTI Act which is to serve public interest. However, efforts have been undertaken by respective CPIOs to provision information whatever permissible and available with them.

Chapter 6
Important Decisions of the Central Information Commission

As brought out earlier, Central Information Commission (CIC) is the highest authority in deciding dispute, appeal or any other issue related to provision of information, hence decisions imparted by the Central Information Commissioner are of paramount importance and forms bench mark for further reference. With this in mind efforts have been undertaken in this chapter to compile some of the important decisions for better appreciation of the provisions of RTI Act; however for details of the relevant decision, readers may like to peruse them in website www. Central Information Commissioner.gov.in as per case reference given at the end of each case.

Prominent Cases. Few prominent cases wherein individuals have filed second appeals to Central Information Commissioner and important decisions given by the commissions have been covered in chapter VI as important decisions of the Central Information Commissioner which would be benchmark for the CPIO/PIO and FAA of the institutes to refer them for suitably disposal of their cases.

Landmark decisions of Central Information Commissioner. Some of the important decisions given by the CIC which pertains to generic and repetitive nature of subjects are enumerated as under:-

Subject	CIC Case Ref	Decision
File Notings	CIC/OK/A/2006/00154 of 13.07.2006	Many Public authorities are denying file notings on the basis of information placed on the DoPT website , despite the fact that the RTI Act does not exempt file notings from disclosure. The commission therefore directed the public authorities (PAs) to furnish the file notings and the concerned ministry to remove the said portion from its website
Language under Section 2 (f)	CIC/WB/A/2006/00117	Jai Kumar applied to Delhi Development Authority asking for information in Hindi as he has applied to the PUBLIC INFORMATION OFFICER in Hindi. The CENTRAL INFORMATION COMMISSIONER directed the DDA to provide the requested information in Hindi within 25 days of the issue of its decision
Citizen under Section 3	CIC/OK/A/2006/00121 – 27 June 2006	PIO can decline information under section 3, if the applicant applies as a Managing Director of a company and not a citizen if India
Address of the Requester	CIC/OK/A/2006/00050 –3 July 2006	The Commission could not agree with the PIO's contention that the information was sought on behalf of an institution. The Appellant has applied in his own name and has only given his address and that of an NGO for the purpose of correct delivery of post. Thus merely giving the address of an NGO does not imply that the institution was asking the information

Subject	CIC Case Ref	Decision
Applicant Seeking Opinions of the Authorities	CIC/MA/A/2006/00150 – 19 June 2006	The PIO is required to 'provide information' which is available in any form with her office rather than giving her personal opinions on the questions asked by the requester
Drafting an application	CIC/OK/A/2006/00 069 of 18.05.2006 & CIC/AT/A/2006/00128 of 13.07.2006	Appeal should be drafted in a simple and direct manner and must be brief. It must not be unnecessarily long, too details and couched in legalese with several repetitions. No fresh grounds for information can be allowed to be urged at appellate levels unless found to be of a nature that would warrant their admittance, if the same has not been brought up at the primary level i.e. PIO level
Personal Discussion with the Requester	CIC/WB/A/2006/00180 of 5 July 2006	If there was general confusion regarding the kind of information that has been called for and that could have been supplied, it could have been easily resolved by a personal sitting between the appellant and the respondents

Due diligence under section 20 (1)	CIC/ AT/A/2006/ 00066	If the time limit could not be adhered to by CPIO, then applicant should be taken in to confidence and periodical progress be apprised to him. (CIC/AT/A/2006/00031 of 10.07.2006.) It may have been lot better if the CPIO had kept the complainant periodically information about the stages of the processing of his case and taken him into confidence about the possibility of some delay. If the time limit could not be adhered to by CPIO, then applicant should be taken in to confidence and periodical progress be apprised to him. (CIC/ AT/A/2006/00031 of 10.07.2006.) It may have been lot better if the CPIO had kept the complainant periodically information about the stages of the processing of his case and taken him into confidence about the possibility of some delay
Answer sheets	ICPB/A-2/ CIC/2006 of 06.02.2006	In case of evaluated answer papers the information is available in fiduciary relationship with the PAs & is exempted under section 8(1) (e). in addition when a candidate seeks for the copy of his / her own or others, it is purely a personal information which has no relationship with any public interest or activities and exempted under section 8(1)(j) of the act. We, as a commission, are not satisfied that larger public interest justifies disclosure of such information. As a matter of fact, we are of the opinion that furnishing copies of the evaluated answer papers would be against the public interest and supply of them would compromise the fairness and impartiality of the selection process.

Cut-Off Marks	180/IC (A)/2006 of 17.08.2006	The commission has directed the Staff Selection Commission to furnish the mark sheets (for written examination as well as interview) to the candidates along with cut-off marks for different categories of candidates.
Marks secured by the candidates	11/53/2006-CIC of 2.5.2006	A division bench has decided that the conduct of examinations are for identifying and short listing the candidates in term of technical competence, the right attitude is highly confidential activities and therefore answer sheets should not be disclosed. But the marks secured by candidates are not to be kept secret and should be disclosed.

Subject	CIC Case Ref	Decision
Annual Confidential Report and Privacy under section 8 (1) (j)	CIC/ AT/A/2006/ 00069 of 13.07.2006	It is our view that what is contained in ACRs is undoubtedly personal information about that employee/ officer. The ACRs are protected from disclosure because arguably such disclosures seriously harm interpersonal relationship in a given organization. Further, the ACRs notings represent an interaction based on the trust and confidence between the officers involved in initiating, reviewing or accepting the ACRs. These officers could be seriously embarrassed and even compromised if their notings are made public. There are thus reasonable grounds to protect all such information through a proper classification under the OSA. No public purpose is going to be served by disclosing this information. On the contrary it may lead to harming the public interest in terms of compromising objectivity of assessment, which is the core and substance of the ACR. This may even result from the uneasiness of the reporting, reviewing or accepting officers from the knowledge that their comments were no longer confidential. These ACRs are used by the PAs for promotions, placements and grading etc. of the officers, which are strictly house keeping and man management functions of any organization. A certain amount of confidentiality insulates these actions from competing pressures and thereby promotes objectivity. We, therefore, are of the view that apart from being personal information, ACRs of officers and employees need not be disclosed because they do not contribute to any public interest. It is also possible that many officers may not like their assessment by their superiors to go into the hands of all and sundry. If the reports are good, these may attract envy and if these are bad, ridicule and derision Either way it affects the employee as well as the organization he/she work for. On balance, therefore, confidentiality of this information serves a larger purpose, which far outstrips the arguments for its disclosures.

Investigating Officer and Privacy	177/IC (A)/2006 – 17 August 2006	A citizen requested from the RBI certain information relating to the findings of an inspection of the Memon Cooperative Bank Limited, Mumbai, which was conducted on the basis of a complaint filed by him and a copy of the inspection report along with the name(s) of the investigating officers. The CIC directed the RBI to furnish a copy of the inspection report after the due application of section 10(1) of the Act. Alternatively, the appellant should be provided a substantive response, incorporating major findings of the inspection report and indicating the action taken on the findings of the report. However, the names of the investigating officers may not be revealed as it would not serve any public interest.
Bio Data and Medical Records under Section 8 (1) (j)	ICPB/A-9/ CIC/2006	Appellant has asked for copies of the bio data submitted by four candidates at the time of their appointment as Assistant Directors and also copies of their medical reports submitted by the medical authorities declaring these candidates fit or unfit. The CIC held that when a candidate submits his application for appointment to a post in a public authority, the same becomes public document and he can not object to the disclosure on the ground of invasion of privacy and directed the PIO to provide copies of the bio data. As far

		as medical reports are concerned, they are purely personal to the individuals and furnishing of the copies of medical reports would amount to invasion of privacy of the individuals and need not be furnished. However, the PIO will disclose to the requester the information whether all four candidates had been declared medically fit or not.
Travel Expenses	63/IC (A)/2006 – 30 March 2006	Travel expenses were charged to the public account. Disclosure of information cannot be denied on the ground of this being personal information and not a public activity and serves no public interest, etc. Travel has been performed as a part and in discharge of official duties and the records related the same are public records and therefore, a citizen has the right to seek disclosure of the same.
Income Tax Returns	22/IC (A)/2006 – 30 March 2006	Income Tax Returns filed by a person are confidential information, which including details of commercial activities and that it relates to the third person. These are submitted in fiduciary capacities. There is no public action involved in the matter. Disclosure is exempted under section 8 (1) (j)

Annual property Returns	CIC/ AT/A/2006/00134 of 10.7.2006	Information in annual property return shall be covered by section 8(1) (j) (h) as well as under section 11 (1) of the act in some cases and cannot be routinely disclosed. However, the PAs are advised to devise a new format so that only such transaction which may not violate the right to privacy can be separated and disclosed.
Period prior to Twenty Years under Section 8 (3)	37/ICPB/2006–26 June 2006	Section 8 (3) is part of section 8, which deals with 'exemption from disclosure of information'. Section 8 (1) specifies classes of information which are exempted from disclosure. What section 8 (3) stipulates is that the exemption under section 8 (1) cannot be applied if the information sought related to a period prior to 20 years except those covered in section clauses (a), (c) and (i) of sub-section 8 (1). In other words, even if the information sought is exempt in terms of other sub-section (1) of section 8, and if the same relates to a period 20 years prior to the date of application, then the same shall be provided.
The Third Party Information	CIC/ WB/A/2006/00051 of 04.07.2006	The RTI Act does not give a third party an automatic veto on disclosure of information. The PIO and AA are required to examine the third party's case in terms of provisions of section 8 (1) (j) or section 11 (1) as the case may be and arrive at the findings by properly assessing the facts and circumstances of the case. A speaking order should thereafter be passed.

| Generating/ Creating Information | 278/IC/(A)2006 of 18.09.2006 | In its oft-repeated decisions, the Commission has advised the information seekers that they ought not to seek the views and comments of the CPIO on the questions asked by them. Yet, in the garb of seeking information mainly for redressal of their grievances, applications from requesters are filed. The CPIO's in turn, have also ventured to answer them. Thus, the information seekers as well as providers have erred in interpreting the definition of information. A CPIO of any public authority is not expected to create and generate fresh information because it has been sought by an appellant. The appellant is, therefore, advised to specify the required information, which may be provided, if it exists, in the form in which it is sought by him. |

Subject	CIC Case Ref	Decision
Seeking view/ opinions of CPIO	69/IC (A) /2006 of 20.06.2006	All the concerned parties were heard and it was noted that there was no question of denial of information. The appellant was however not satisfied because he sought 'opinion' of the CPIO through a long list of queries, which is not covered under the definition of information. However, the information, which was clearly specified, was provided to him.

Seeking interpretation of rule/ Law	CIC/AT/A/2006/ 00185 of 18.09.2006	Before parting with this appeal, it must be pointed out that this is the first time a party has come up to the Commission asking for interpretation of a given / rules as well as the interpretation of the powers of a quasi-judicial body. As I stated in the first appeal, the proper Forum test the order of a Tribunal is as laid down under the appropriate Act or as provided in the Constitution. It would be wholly inappropriate to invoke the provisions of the RTI Act for the interpretation of laws and rules. It should be made clear that the laws and rules are themselves 'information' and being in public domain are accessible to all citizens of the country.
Form of Access under Section 2 (f)	10/01/2005-CIC – 25 February 2006	If the requested information is not available in electronic form as requested by the requester, if does not have to be created for the appellant. (CIC/MA/A/2006/0002 – 27 June 2006) If the information is not available in the particular form requested, the citizen may be allowed, if he desires, to inspect the original records at the office and information specifically asked for provided in the form of printouts and photocopies of original documents and records duly certified.
Information held under Section 2 (j)	CIC/ AT/A/2006/20 – 23 March 2006	In this case records of the court martial trial were destroyed after a retention period of 10 years under the Army Rule 146. Information did not exist, it was physically impossible to provide it. There is no liability under the RTIA on a public authority to supply non-existent information.

Voluntary Disclosure under Section 4 (1) (b)	24/IC(A)/2006 –16 April 2006	A public authority, is required to make pro-active disclosure of all the relevant information as per provisions of section 4 (1) (b) unless the same is exempt under the provisions of section 8 (1). In fact on information regime should be create such that citizens would have easy access to information without making any formal request for it.
Record Management under section 4 (1) (a)	CIC/OK/ A/2006/00016-15.6.06	Record management system ought to be improved such that information which is to be disclosed could be easily provided after delineating those that is exempted.
Consultation between the President and the Supreme Court	CIC/ AT/A/2006/00113 of 10.07.2006)	The Central Information Commissioner concluded that the entire process of consultation between the President of India and the Supreme Court under article 124(2) is exempted under section 8(1) (e) and 11(1) of the RTI Act.

Subject	CIC Case Ref	Decision
Public Interest and Consumer Protection	37/IC (A)/2006 – 12 May 2006	Appellant has made the case of public interest on the grounds of adulteration in distribution of diesel and petrol. He has however not substantiated his point as to how he would prove his allegations on the basis of disclosure of income tax returns filed by the third party. Apparently there is no direct relationship between malpractices of petrol and diesel and income tax returns, which is mainly the basis for seeking information.
High Court's stay on the CIC's Decision	CIC/MA/ A/2006/0012-1- 8 August 2006	For the first time after the enactment of the RTI Act, Delhi High Court issued stay on a decision taken by the CIC. Delhi High Court on 22 August 2006 stayed the CIC decision directing the government to make available to it copies of the late President K. R. Narayanan's letters written to the then Prime Minister Atal Bihari Vajpayee relating to 2002 communal violence in Gujarat. Justice Anil Kumar stayed 8 August 2006 order till 11 January 2007 on an application moved by the Union Government saying that the letters could not be made available to the CIC as it would impinge on the national security and integrity.

Compensation to the Applicants	CIC/ WB/C/2006/00145 - 10 August 2006	Misbehavior with applicants approaching public authorities under the RTI is not acceptable and is violation of section 5 (3). In this case the PUBLIC INFORMATION OFFICER will invite Ms. Dasharathi to visit his office and identify members of his staff who refused to provide her the information. Under section 19 (8) (b) the public authority will pay Rs. 100 as damages suffered to the applicant Ms. Dasharathi. This may be either directly or through recovery from the erring officials, as deemed appropriate by the PIO.
Compensation under Section 19(8) (b)		For the first time, the CIC in its decision directed the Central Government Health Scheme, Pune to pay a sum of Rs. 5,000 to the appellant Ms. M. N. Trival as compensation and refund her the sum of Rs.60 paid by her as fee for non-application of mind by both the PIO and AA resulted in the appellant's having to interact with PIO and CIC repeatedly causing mental harassment to her.

Penalty Under Section 20(1)	CIC/ WB/C/2006/00040	For the first time, Shri Wajahat Habibullah, Chief Information Commissioner imposed a penalty of Rs. 25,000 on a Public Information Officer for a complaint number CIC/WB/C/2006/00040, 5 June, 2006. Public Information Officer (PIO) has failed to appear before the commission on due date and time despite a telephone reminder. Because the burden of proving that he acted reasonably and diligently is on the PIO under Provision II to Sec 20(1), it is assumed that he has no reasonable cause to show why penalty should not be imposed. Under the aforementioned section of the Act, penalty shall be imposed on any of the grounds, (a) if the PIO has refused to receive an application or (b) not furnished the information within the time frame specified in section 7 (1) or (c) malafidely denied the request for information or knowingly given incorrect information. The PIO is in violations of above not to provide the information sought and also obstructed the complainant's, he will therefore pay a penalty of Rs. 250 for every day subject to a maximum of Rs. 25,000.

Subject	CIC Case Ref	Decision
Failure to assist the Commission	CIC/WB/C/ 2006/00040	The Commissioner of Municipal Corporation Delhi has failed to assist the Commission, which he was legally bound to do, and he also failed to explain as to why the orders of this Commission were not executed. It also appears that he has thereby caused an interruption to the proceedings. He has, therefore, committed offences punishable under section 176, 187, 188 and 228 of Indian Panel Code. Now therefore, it is ordered as follows: That the commissioner, MCD shall appear in person on 18 August 2006 at 10:30 AM and show cause (a) As to why he be not prosecuted for committing the said offences and (b) As to why appropriate action be not recommended against him under section 20(2) of the Right to information Act; and (c) As to why such further action or actions be not taken as this commission may deem fit and proper. He further directed to furnish the names and address of the concerned CPIO(s) who were responsible for not furnishing the information to the appellant so as to enable initiation of appropriate proceedings against them.

Penalty under Section 20(1)	CIC/OK/ C/2006/00042-28July 2006	Commission imposed a penalty of Rs. 13,750 on professor Akthar Majeed, registrar, Jamia Hamdard, New Delhi . The commission further authorized and requested the Vice Chancellor, Jamia Hamdard, New Delhi to cause the recovery of the amount of penalty from the salary of Professor Akhtar Majeed and remit the amount by demand draft or banker's cheque drawn in favour of Pay and Account Officer, DP&AR, payable at New Delhi, to Shri Pankaj K.P. Shreyaskar, assistant Registrar, Central information Commission, 4th Floor, Block No. IV, Old J.N.U. Campus, New Delhi-110067, by 15 September 2006.
Penalty of Rs. 25000 imposed	CIC/ OK/A/2006/ 00163 of 19.10.2006	In exercise of powers conferred by Sec. 20(1) of the RTI Act 2005, the Commission imposes a penalty of Rs.25,000/- (Rupees twenty five thousand only) on Shri N. Sundaram, Registrar, BHU for denial of information despite the Commission's clear directions and directs him to remit the penalty by D.D. in favour of the Pay & Accounts Officer, DP&AR, payable at New Delhi, to Shri Pankaj KP. Shreyaskar, Assistant Registrar, CIC, within 15 days of issue of this order. In case of failure, the VC has been authorized to recover the amount from the salary of Shri Sundaram, and deposit the amount with CIC on or before 15.11.2006.

Disciplinary Action under Section 20(2)	CIC/MA/A/2006/00012- 10 March 2006	The CIC recommended disciplinary action against an appellate officer. The appellate authority is not covered under the penal provisions of the Act. But in this case, he clearly failed to uphold the act in the public interest. It was observed that this decision may be sent to public authority to consider disciplinary action under their service rules. CIC/EB/C/2006/00040-24 April 2006 Commercial Secrets Protected by Law under Section 8(1) (d) and 11(1)A request was received by the Chief Commissioner of Customs for the names of importers and exporters in daily list of import and export which are being published from the custom houses. But a notification No. 128/2004-Cus (NT) dated 19 November 2004 forbids the disclosure of the names requested. The CIC held that the notification containing rules are in the nature of subordinate legislation is appropriate under section 8(1) (d) of the RTI Act .

Contract Under Section 8(1)) (d)	CIC/WB/C/2006/00176-18 April 2006	Ramesh Chand applied to National Institute of Science Communication and Information and sought information on terms of the conditions and their implementation regarding a contract with another firm. The CIC held that a contract with a public authority is not confidential. Offer, completion, quotations, bid, tender, prior to conclusion of a contract can be categorized as trade secret, but once concluded, the confidentiality of such transactions con not be claimed. Any public authority claims exemption must be put to strictest proof that exemption is justifiably claimed. Therefore, this public authority was directed to disclose the list of employees.

Few important second appeal cases filed at the office of the Central Information Commission and decisions given wherein information is considered to be closely related to Armed Forces are enumerated in succeeding paragraphs.

(a) **Anomaly in pension to widow of a deceased officer.**

  (i) **Information Sought.** Appellant had sought information re-garding the authority responsible for communicating the attribute factor to the pension fixation of the time frame and requested for copy of letter under which her pension was fixed as 'Ordinary Family Pension' as against 'Special Family Pension'.

(ii) **Action of CPIO/AA.** Information available on record was provisioned to the appellant by CPIO and queries not pertaining to this headquarter transferred to other Central Public Information Officer/Public Information Officer. First Appellate Authority upheld the decision of CPIO.

(iii) **Decision of CIC.** The CIC was informed that case is of old vintage and the files have been weeded out. However, CIC asked the CPIO to revisit the matter and provide information whatsoever available.

(b) **Information pertaining to CSD and URCs.**

(i) **Information Sought.** Appellant had sought information on consolidated profit energized from 3500 CSD canteens as on 31 Mar 2008 and information on mallied issues.

(ii) **Action of CPIO/AA.** Part of information was provisioned to appellant by CPIO. The appellant was also informed that details/data on URC profits are not maintained centrally and would result in disproportionate use of Government resources in provisioning of information sought. First Appellate Authority affirmed the decision of Central Public Information Officer.

(iii) **Decision of CIC.** CIC affirmed the position taken by CPIO for not providing information regarding turnover and profit generated by URCs operated in the Army System, as URCs are private entities which cannot be treated as a public authority.

(c) **Nomination for Higher Command Course.**

(i) **Information Sought.** Appellant a serving officer had sought information pertaining to officers considered for nomination to Higher Command and equivalent courses in 2008, 2009 and 2010 and recommendations of the board of officers.

(ii) **Action by CPIO/AA** Available and permissible information was provided by the CPIO. First Appellate Authority affirmed the decision of CPIO.

(iii) **Decision of CIC.** After having seen the board proceedings, CIC observed that the closed door proceedings were held and the names of candidates were not put up before the screening committee. Even otherwise commission is not competent to go into the relative of merits of the candidates and the methodology of selection adopted by the screening committee. Appeal was dismissed.

(d) **Copies of Strength Return Officers (IAFF-3008) and Part II Orders.**

(i) **Information Sought**. The appellant sought copies of Strength return Officers other than JCOs/PBOR and copies of Part II Orders of a unit from Jan 2002 to Jul 2002.

(ii) **Action by CPIO/AA**. Provisioning of information was denied to appellant by CPIO under sec 8(1)(a) of RTI Act05 . First Appellate Authority upheld the decision of CPIO and rejected the appeal.

(iii) **Decision of CIC**. CIC was apprised that appellant being serving personnel may seek information through departmental channel after justifying reasons for obtaining such information as the provision exist for the same. CPIO also brought out that since requested information involve holding strength of a unit hence disclosure through the instrumentality of RTI act is not appropriate. CIC endorsed decision taken by CPIO and disposed off the appeal.

(e) **Premature retirement.**

(i) **Information Sought.** The appellant' son a serving officer in the Army, had applied for PMR which was turned down. Appellant sought information wrt data on life status of parents of officers who had proceeded on PMR and grounds on which other officers were released from the service and misc infor-mation on related issues.

(ii) **Action by CPIO**. CPIO provisioned the available informa-tion to the appellant. The appellant did not prefer 1st appeal and filed 2nd appeal to the CIC.

(iii) **Decision of CIC** The CIC affirmed the stand of CPIO that the Army is not maintaining any such data base, hence appeal was dismissed accordingly.

(f) Disparity in Promotion Board No 2 Selection Board.

(i) **Information Sought.** Appellant had sought copies of noting, policy letters and information regarding policy decisions to maintain batch parity in 2 Selection Boards amongst all arms & services with special reference to a minor Corps.

(ii) **Action by CPIO/AA.** CPIO provisioned the available infor-mation to the appellant, however justifications / clarifications sought were denied to appellant. First Appellate Authority af-firmed the decision of CPIO.

(iii) **Decision of CIC.** CIC mentioned in his order that in his opin-ion, it is essentially a policy matter which is to be looked into by concerned Directorate / Ministry. He further recorded that as the appellant has not sought any specific information, the matter be treated as closed.

(g) Procedure for contractual employment of staff for ECHS Poly-clinics.

(i) Information Sought. Appellant had sought information re-garding the functioning of ECHS vis-à-vis that of CGHS and issues concerning working hours and leave entitlement etc.

(ii) Action by CPIO/AA. CPIO provisioned part of information to the appellant. At appeal stage, First Appellate Authority directed CPIO to respond to some of the queries are not re-sponded earlier, which was complied with.

(iii) Decision of CIC. CIC noticed that the appellant has raised establishment related issues which though important, do not appear to fall in the ambit of RTI Act 05 and the appeal was dismissed.

(h) Use of armed forces during Communal Violence.

    (i) **Information Sought.** Appellant had sought information as to whether any Executive Magistrate or Commission or a Gazetted member of Armed Forces exercised his/her powers to disperse an assembly using the Armed Forces under his or her command under section 130 and 131 of the Criminal Procedure Code 1973 respectively, pertaining to communal violence at certain places.

    (ii) **Action by CPIO/AA.** CPIO informed the appellant that part of the information will be provided by the concerned PIO of subordinate formations headquarters of the Army and the appellant was also informed that the details of Magistrates involved in such operations are not held with the Army. First Appellate Authority directed appellant to approach respective state government to ascertain details asked.

    (iii) **Decision of CIC.** CIC agreed with the CPIO for difficulties in collecting and collating the information asked, however, CIC opined that information requested is not barred f r o m disclosure under the provision of the RTI Act 05 and directed that efforts be undertaken by Army auth to obtain requisite information in 10 weeks time and be fwd to appellant.

(j) Withholding of DV Clearance for promotion.

    (i) **Information Sought.** The appellant had sought copy of policies at Army headquarter as on 14 Sep 2007 regarding withholding of DV Clearance for stopping promotion after he has been empanelled for promotion and misc information pertaining to related issues.

    (ii) **Action by CPIO/AA.** CPIO provisioned the available information to the appellant. First Appellate Authority affirmed the decision of CPIO.

    (iii) **Decision of CIC.** The CIC in his order stated that the request for provisioning of file notings relating to the initiation of process leading to the imposition of DV ban on the appellant be provisioned to him after obliterating the names and designation of the officers under section 10(1) of the RTI Act 05.

(k) Use of official facilities for the families of Army pers.

    (i) **Information Sought.** The appellant had sought information whether Army personnel are entitled to use official facilities like vehicle, phone, orderlies etc for the families and information on related issues.

    (ii) **Action by CPIO/AA.** Part of the information was provisioned to the appellant by CPIO and part information was denied being hypothetical in nature. First Appellate Authority affirmed the decision of CPIO and directed the appellant to ask for specific information through a fresh application addressed to CPIO.

    (iii) **Decision of CIC.** CIC directed the CPIO to revisit the matter and obtain and provide additional information to the appellant. Balance available information was provisioned to the appellant.

(l) ACR details & misc Queries.

    (i) **Information Sought.** The appellant, a retired officer had sought information in respect of ACRs for the years 2003 to 2008, including the numerical grading awarded and other information on other such matters.

    (ii) **Action by CPIO/AA.** Some of the permissible information was provisioned to appellant by CPIO and part information was denied under section 8(1)(e) & 8(1)(j) of RTI Act 05. First Appellate Authority affirmed the decision of CPIO.

    (iii) **Decision of CIC.** Quoting Honorable Supreme Court judgment in Dev Dutt Vs UOI case under which ACR grading of service personnel is debarred to be given , the CIC upheld the decision of the CPIO, and further said appeal has no merit and the same was dismissed.

(m) Copy of Decision and other issues pertaining to Court Martial.

(i) **Information Sought.** The appellant a retired service personnel requested for provisioning of a copy of the decision announced by the GCM in response to his plea in bar along with the reasons recorded by the General Court Martial as announced in open court. He also further requested to furnish a copy of the noting sheet / recommendations of the General Officer Commanding-in-Chief of concerned Command Headquarter while forwarding the case for appropriate orders to confirming authority.

(ii) **Action by CPIO/AA.** Provisioning of information was denied to appellant by the CPIO under sec 8(1) (h) of RTI Act 05. However the First Appellate Authority after going through the details directed the concerned Directorate to procure part of the information from the concerned Command Headquarter and provide the same. This also could not be done since appellant had filed a case later in the court and information sought had direct relevance with the court case.

(iii) **Decision of CIC.** CIC remanded the appeal back to the First Appellate Authority for making a clear decision on the case. First Appellate Authority re-heard the case and stated that information requested for is exempt from provisioning under sec 8(1)(h) and 8(1)(e) of RTI Act 05. CIC fixed up second hearing of the case and summoned CPIO and officer in charge of files to be present with related files/ records pertaining to the issue. Besides CPIO, legal representative of the JAG branch were in attendance. After due deliberations, CIC opined that appellant is fully entitled to information and hence ordered that the conclusion of GCM proceeding contained in five pages of the proceedings be fwd to appellant.

(n) Information pertaining to CSD and URCs.

(i) Information Sought. Appellant had sought information on

consolidated profit energized from 3500 CSD canteens as on 31 Mar 2008 and information on allied issues.

(ii) Action by CPIO/AA.. Part of information was provisioned to appellant by CPIO. The appellant was also informed that details/data on URC profits are not maintained centrally and would result in disproportionate use of Government resources in provisioning of information. First Appellate Authority affirmed the decision of CPIO.

(iii) Decision of CIC. IC inclined with the position taken by CPIO for not providing information regarding turnover and profit generated by URCs operated in the Army system, as URCs are private entities which do not fall in public domain and dismissed the appeal.

(o) **Granting permanent commission to officer of Army Dental Corps.**

(i) Information Sought. Appellant had requested for provisioning of copies of mark sheet, selection board proceedings and related information pertaining to the special board which was convened to consider case for grant of permanent commission in the Army Dental Corps.

(ii) Action by CPIO/AA. Part of the information was provisioned to appellant by CPIO and part information was denied under section 8 (1)(j) and 8(1)(e) of RTI Act 05. First Appellate Authority directed CPIO to provision additional information which was also provided to the appellant.

(iii) Decision of CIC . CIC directed CPIO to provision the marks awarded by the Selection Board for award of permanent commission after applying the severability clause and also intimate to the appellant whether there was any adverse remarks in CRs for the entire service period.

(p) **Provisioning of sample of Sleeping Bag.**

(i) **Information Sought.** Appellant requested for perusal of sample marked G2 (Sleeping Bag with Cover of M/S Moncler, Franch which was fwd to a particular formation, in the office of concerned Directorate of Integrated Headquarters of Ministry of Defence (Army).

(ii) **Action by CPIO/AA.** CPIO afforded adequate opportunity to the appellant to inspect the sample and informed him to contact the concerned Branch at certain location to inspect the sample which was done by the appellant. First Appellate Authority affirmed the decision of CPIO.

(iii) **Decision of CIC.** Appellant submitted that he is interested in sample G2. It was apprised to CIC that sample which was available with the Pubic Authority has already been shown to appellant. CIC directed the CPIO to make fresh efforts to trace out the sample marked G-2 and if the same is traced out the appellant may be allowed to inspect it. However, if the sample has been destroyed, the appellant may be given a copy of the destruction certificate.

(iv) In this instant case, later, a copy of destruction cert was fwd to appellant.

(q) Person with Disabilities

(i) **Information Sought.** Appellant had sought information whether the provisions of Para 47 of the Persons with Disabilities (Equal Opportunities, Protection of Rights and Full Participation Act, 1995 are applicable to the Indian Army and requested for provisioning of copy of amendments made if any.

(ii) **Action by CPIO/AA.** The CPIO intimated the appellant that requested information is ready for provisioning and same would be provisioned to him/her on receipt of information material charges. First Appellate Authority endorsed the decision of CPIO and asked appellant to collect the information after making prescribed payment as per the Act.

(iii) **Decision of CIC.** CIC in his decision stated that the Public Authority has no objection to provide requisite information.

The only question is non-payment of the requisite fee by the appellant. Hence, in exercise of its plenary powers, the commission waives off the fee and directed CPIO to supply the requisite information to the appellant, which was later fwd to appellant.

(r) Copy of Medical examination report at the time of commissioning

(i) **Information Sought.** The appellant an estranged wife of a serving officer, had sought a copy of Medical and health status report filled in the form by her husband at the time of entry into the Army.

(ii) **Action by CPIO/AA .** Provisioning of information was denied by CPIO under sec 8(1)(j) of RTI Act 05 being third party information and consent of serving officer was also not to share the information. First Appellate Authority upheld the decision of CPIO through speaking order.

(iii) **Decision of CIC.** Even though the third party i.e. serving officer has declined to give consent to part with information, the CIC directed the CPIO to apply severability clause u/s 10 (1) of the RTI Act 05 and supply information only in regard to one of the query pertaining to health status of his mother filled in by the serving officer at the time of joining Army.

(s) Information regarding martyrs permanently disabled & injured during wars.

(i) **Information Sought.** Appellant had sought information regarding number of brave soldiers martyred, permanently disabled and injured since 1947 onwards in various war/ops/conflict.

(ii) **Action by CPIO/AA .** Provisioning the information was denied to appellant by the CPIO under sec 8(1)(a) of RTI Act 05 stating that information sought is classified in nature. FAA affirmed the decision of CPIO.

(iii) **Decision of CIC .** Though CIC was in agreement with decision of the CPIO, however he further felt that Ministry of Defence appears to be the proper agency to take a stance on the matter. Hence, CPIO of Ministry of Defence is hereby directed to send a formal response to the appellant in 4 weeks time.

(t) Details of Construction and purchase of various items for Furnishing

(i) Information Sought. The appellant had requested for numerous information in relation to a work undertaken at Delhi Cantt like purchase of products/items/orders, their cost, sanction, funds, payments etc and into on related matters.

(ii) Action by CPIO/AA. CPIO provisioned available and permissible information to the appellant. First Appellate Authority directed CPIO to also provide balance information as has been recd from concerned headquarters to the appellant.

(iii) Decision of CIC . CIC after carefully examining the proceeding of the case stated that the appellant has mentioned that the CPIO has not supplied him complete and proper information, however, he has not specified as to how and why the information is not complete and proper. CIC further noted that the appellant has not appeared before the Commission to canvass his case. The case was dismissed by CIC as devoid of merit in the appeal.

(u) Correspondence regarding Recruitment of a JCO.

(i) **Information Sought.** The appellant had requested for provisioning of copy of complaint submitted against rejection of his application for screening as recruit of JCO (RT) course.

(ii) **Action by CPIO/AA.** CPIO informed the appellant that documents asked have been destroyed as per rule in vogue being more than 03 years old and the same could not be provided. First Appellate Authority directed CPIO to fwd relevant extract of Board of Officers regarding destruction of documents pertaining to points raised by appellant.

(iii) **Decision of CIC.** CIC in his decision stated that whatever documents were available with the public authority had already been provided to the appellant and the rest of the documents could not be supplied as these were reportedly weeded out. He further mentioned that unending correspondence with this Commission, including telephonic calls from appellant are viewed adversely and the matter stands closed at Commission's end.

(v) Investigation of Navy War Room Leak by CBI

(i) **Information Sought.** Appellant had sought information in r/o raids conducted on 26 Jun 2006 by CBI during investigations of the Navy War Room Leak, including forwarding of names and ranks of the officers raided with their units.

(ii) **Action by CPIO/AA.** CPIO advised appellant to seek the requisite information directly from the CBI as CBI has specifically stipulated that SP's report/any information shared, be treated as a confidential document and in case anybody seeks a copy or part thereof under RTI Act 05, the CBI should be consulted before deciding the matter. First Appellate Authority directed the concerned branch to seek clearance from CBI for provisioning of information to the appellant.

(iii) **Decision of CIC.** CIC in his order stated that SP's report requested for by the appellant is not to be disclosed u/s 8(1)(h) of RTI Act 2005. However, CBI is hereby directed to provide a copy of the order of the Supreme Court on the subject to the appellant.

(w) Copy of Noting on Posting of Serving Army officer

(i) **Information Sought.** The appellant a serving officer had requested for provisioning of noting sheets and related documents pertaining to his posting and cancellation thereof.

(ii) **Action by CPIO/AA.** Some of the generic nature of information sought was provisioned to the appellant, however copy of notings were denied. First Appellate Authority affirmed the decision of CPIO.

(iii) **Decision of CIC.** After due deliberations CIC observed that denial of notings on the subject is not appropriate by CPIO, hence directed to furnish requisite information including file notings to the appellant.

(x) Proof of Citizenship

(i) **Information Sought.** The appellant had sought copies of Government orders/notification and/or document authorising demand of a photo identity with each request/application under the RTI Act 05 and also requested for provisioning of information related to DNB-Super specialty course 2008-10 which was held at Army Hosp (R&R).

(ii) **Action by CPIO/AA.** In reply to the initial query of appellant, the CPIO intimated to appellant that Sec 3 of RTI Act 05 states that right to information under this Act extends to Indian citizens only. As CPIO does not hold records of any citizen and deals with sensitive issues , a proof of Citizenship is solicited to ensure that information is provided to Indian citizens only and do not find its way to wrong hands. The appellant preferred 2nd appeal before the CIC w/o preferring first appeal.

(iii) **Decision of CIC.** CIC in his decision stated that he had no doubt that information can be sought only by an Indian citizen under section 3 of the RTI Act. Further he stated that furnishing of such proof before the CPIO may be cumbersome and may involve costs and delays. To deprive such individuals of their statutory right would not be just, fair and equitable. CIC opined that the proof of citizenship is not required from an information seeker as a matter of principle. However, in certain exceptional circumstances, where the CPIO, particularly of the Armed Forces, have a doubt about the citizenship of the information seeker, it is open to seek proof of citizenship.

(y) Copy of Permission obtained for taking up a job post retirement

(i) **Information Sought.** Appellant had sought information to know whether a particular retired officer of Indian Army had sought permission from the competent Army authority as per rules before taking up a job with other agencies after his retirement.

(ii) **Action by CPIO/AA.** The information sought was denied to appellant by the CPIO u/s 8(1)(e) & 8(1)(j) of RTI Act 05. FAA affirmed the decision of CPIO.

(iii) **Decision of CIC.** CIC placed it on record that the denial of information on the ground of the requested information being kept in fiduciary capacity is not sustainable in law. However, since public authority is not retaining the relevant records, appellant to be informed accordingly. Since no information on the subject available with the pubic authority, appeal has become purely of an academic interest and the matter was accordingly closed.

(z) Information on Army Welfare Housing Organisation (AWHO)

(i) **Information Sought.** Appellant had sought information regarding area occupied, rent, electricity and water charges paid by the AWHO, details of combatant employees, their salaries, audits carried out and role of Ministry of Defence pertaining to AWHO etc.

(ii) **Action by CPIO/AA.** CPIO informed the appellant that AWHO is not a public authority and doesn't come under the provisions of the RTI Act 05. The appellant did not prefer 1st appeal and filed 2nd appeal at the office of CIC.

(iii) **Decision of CIC.** CIC did mention in his decision that AWHO is not a public authority under section 2 (h) of the RTI Act 05, however, if there is some information available with the CPIO or with the Army authorities, the same shall certainly be made available by the concerned CPIO u/s 2(j) of the Act. Accordingly, some of the generic information was provisioned to the appellant.

(aa) Copies of ACRs of Retired Service Personnel

(i) **Information Sought.** The appellant a retired JCO had requested for copies of his ACRs for years 1983 to 1992. The application was transferred to concerned Records with policy on disclosure of ACRs under RTI Act 05.

(ii) **Action by CPIO/AA.** PIO of the concerned Records Office not divulged the information sought as copies of ACRs of service personnel are not been provisioned under RTI Act 05 and also do not serve any public interest.

(iii) **Decision of CIC.** After due deliberation and hearing the contention of CPIO, the CIC to an extent agreed that providing copies of ACR to a retired personnel is a burdensome affair. He however, in his order mentioned that overall grading given by the IO, RO and SRO, may be communicated to the requester, entire copies of the ACRs need not be supplied. He also mentioned that information on grading of ACR for the last five years of the retired service personnel can be provided and the subject information be provisioned to the appellant after a gap of 03 years from the date of retirement.

(ab) Merit List : SSB

(i) **Information Sought.** The appellant had sought copy of merit list of 12 and 13 TES 2005 course, display of merit list on the website of Army & reasons for withdrawal of the same from website and information on related issues.

(ii) **Action by CPIO/AA.** Available and permissible information was provisioned to the appellant by the CPIO. The appellant did not prefer 1st appeal and filed 2nd appeal before the CIC.

(iii) **Decision of CIC.** The Army being a sensitive organization, nothing should be done to tinker with its morale and service environment. Further, CIC mentioned that he seems no compelling reasons to deviate from the Army's prevailing practice of non-disclosure of comparative merit. In the circumstances, it will suffice if the total marks obtained in SSB are disclosed to him and this will not be cited as a precedent is also placed on record.

(ac) Information on Selection Boards for Promotion

(i) **Information Sought.** Appellant had sought copies of agenda and the convening order for SSB of a batch along with No 1 SB for another batch held in Jan 2009 and information related to Master Data Sheet (MDS) maintained by Military Secretary Branch of the Army..

(ii) **Action by CPIO/AA.** CPIO provisioned available and permissible information to the appellant. First Appellate Authority directed CPIO to provide additional information as recd from concerned Directorate to the appellant. The same was provisioned to the appellant accordingly.

(iii) **Decision of CIC.** CIC observed that the adequate information has already been provisioned to the appellant. However, CIC directed the CPIO to confirm whether 'Internal Assessment' and 'Integrity Checks' are one activity and communicate the same to the appellant in writing. CPIO in consultations with MS branch of the Army confirmed to the appellant that no record of internal assessment carried out for the Selection Boards are currently maintained.

Chapter 7
Case Studies

Few prominent RTI cases wherein outcome of decisions given by the CIC or the court had made affect on the handling of RTI cases with the Armed Forces are illustrated below as case studies:-

(a) Case No 1

CIC/LS/A/2012/001662

Subject : Copies of CRs

Background of the Case

Appellant a retired service officer of the rank of Maj Gen had asked for copies of each of the CR/ICR earned in the rank of Maj Gen from the CPIO of Army Headquarters. CPIO has replied to the appellant stating "CRs of Military Officers are considered protected information hence exempted from disclosure under RTI Act 2005. In this context, there are numerous decisions of the Central Information Commission available in public domain and appellant may refer these." Aggrieved with the decision of the CPIO, appellant filed first appeal wherein First Appellate Authority affirmed the decision of the CPIO. Second appeal filed by the appellant was heard on 24 July 12 and based on plea by CPIO and representative of MS branch, the hearing of the case was adjourned to 24 Aug 12. Meanwhile as directed by the honorable Central Information Commissioner, A written representation was submitted to their office, wherein reasons for denial of copies of CR/ ICR to retired officer were given as Increase in workload, Increase in litigation, adverse impact on objective reporting, interventions in CRs likely to be questioned, Compliant Against officers in Service, Dissatisfaction amongst Retired Officers Fraternity, CRs in Fiduciary Relationship, Alternate Remedies Available and change in Status of Protection of CR from disclosure.

Deliberations

The issue was deliberated at the office of the Central Information Commissioner on 24 Aug 12. A previous decision on case No CIC/ LS/A/2009/001062 of appellant Shri Yudhvir Singh (A retired JCO from Army) was also referred wherein Central Information Commissioner has ordered CPIO "In case copies of CR available then provision overall grading of IO, RO and SRO for last 5 years of service and only after gap of 3 years of retirement". Keeping in view of the importance of the issues involved, Information Commissioner, Shri ML Sharma requested for constituting a full bench to hear and decide the matter on 04 Dec 12. Accordingly the issue came up for hearing on 04 Dec 12 by full bench of the Central Information Commissioner comprising of Ms A Dixit, Shri ML Sharma and Shri Vijay Sharma. Appellant made forceful attack on present system of initiating/reviewing of CRs of Army Officers stating it is defective and resulted in unsuitable officers being promoted to the superior positions. However, the commission had opined that it cannot comment on the efficacy of present system of writing/reviewing of CRs of Army officers. This legitimately falls in the domain of Army headquarter/MoD. Further, the commission refers following:-

-    Supreme Court decision in the case of Dev Dutt which expressly barred disclosure of CRs

-    Recent DoPT's stance wherein a revision of instructions on disclosure of CRs.

-    Decisions given by CIC in cases no CIC/AT/2006/00069 and CIC/SM/ A/2009/ 00112/LS wherein disclosure of CRs under the Act was denied.

-    Army Instructions 1989

Full Bench Decision of the CIC

Though it has been observed that the views taken in most of the cases referred above are of serving officer and not retired officer, however, the commission is of the opinion that if full details of CRs are disclosed to the retired officer, it may adversely affect their inter personal relationship and result in breach of camaraderie. Further, such disclosure may also result in finger pointing and vitiate atmosphere amongst the fraternity of retired officers. More importantly, such disclosure may also have an adverse impact on objective reporting which is the sine qua non for the efficient functioning of military machine. Disclosure may also result in unacceptable increase of workload of the MS branch of the Army. Hence this bench of the commission approves single bench decision dated 09 Mar 10 in the case No CIC/LS/A/2009/001062 of appellant Shri Yudhvir Singh, which provides for conditional/limited disclosure of CRs to retired personnel. In the instant case appellant does not meet the criteria since three years have not lapsed since his retirement, therefore not entitled to even conditional/limited disclosure. We therefore constrained to dismiss the appeal.

(b) Case No 2

CIC/SM/A/2009/00493 dated 27.11.2008, CIC/LS/A/2010/001518 dated 22.11.2010 and 27.12.10.

Subject : Copies of Court of Inquiry including findings and applicability of RTI act in J&K.

Background of the Case

Under the RTI Act 2005, applicant wife of a senior serving officer of the rank of Maj Gen in the Army vide her application in Nov 2008 has sought attested copies of complete Court of Inquiry report including findings ordered against her husband at Headquarters of Infantry Division in Northern Sector. The inquiry was ordered to investigate the circumstances under which a lady officer was sexually harassed and criminal force was used to outrage her modesty. Appellant also sought following documents:-

- Copies of in & out register of Headquarter Command and Headquarter Corps from 01 Aug 2007 to 31 Mar 2008.

- Attested copies of office file dealing with the disciplinary case of my husband at headquarter command.

- Attested copies of office file dealing with the disciplinary case of her husband at headquarter Northern Comd.

- Certified copy of the order converting the Summary General Court Martial to General Court Martial.

- Copy of the cancellation order of Summary General Court Martial.

- Copy of File pertaining to processing of statutory complaint initiated by her husband with its noting between Army headquarter and MoD.

Processing of the Case and Deliberations

The application was transferred to Headquarter Northern Command for directly provision of information to the appellant under sec 6(3) of RTI Act. As regard to copy of file related to processing of statutory complaint Discipline and vigilance Directorate of the Army provisioned information in Dec 2008. In the meantime, Concerned Headquarter Corps located in J&K apprised the applicant that as per Section 1 (2) of RTI Act 2005, the provision of ibid Act is not applicable in J&K State. Hence information sought cannot be provisioned. Appellate preferred first appeal before the Appellate Authority of Army Headquarters stating that misleading information has been provisioned and also highlighted the issues endorsing a CIC decision wherein an appeal pertaining to RTI Act being applicable in J&K was accepted. The appeal was disposed off by the First Appellate Authority trough a Speaking Order wherein he upheld the decision of the CPIO. Aggrieved by the decision of the First Appellate Authority, the applicant has preferred second appeal before the Honorable CIC. CIC heard the case on 27 Mar 09 and directed the CPIO to reconsider his decision within 15 working days from receipt of this order and directed CPIO to either provide the information sought excluding the report of the Court of Inquiry or if it to be denied, then it should be trough a proper speaking order giving the legal basis for denying any such information. FAA of concerned HQ reiterated his stance of 'RTI Act not applicable to units/formations of the Army located in J&K', hence denied the information sought. Later applicant filed petition at Delhi High Court and stay on the decision of CIC was ordered by the High Court, as a similar case filed by Mrs Veena Kohli was also under consideration at Delhi High Court, wherein the mother of deceased son had requested some piece of information from the unit, located in the State of J&K. Both cases were heard on 28 Jul 2010 at the Delhi High Court, wherein the Honorable Court ordered the Army to provision the requisite information within 15 days and stay on applicability of RTI Act to the units located in the State of J&K was vacated. Based on said decision, despite advisory by RTI cell of army Headquarters to provision information forthwith, the Public Information Officer of Headquarter Corps again denied the information under the garb of section 8 (1) (a) & (e) of RTI Act 2005. Applicant again moved to Honorable CIC complaining non receipt of information from the public authority. And accordingly case was rescheduled for hearing on 22 Nov 2010.

Decision of CIC

During the hearing, the PIO objected to disclose the information to the applicant as no such practice in Army is followed to disclose the contents of a file to the civilian. Based on comments submitted by the PIO, the Honorable CIC directed the Public Information Officer to produce the files before him and the case was adjourned to 27 Dec 12. Later on 27 Dec 10, wherein the Honorable CIC perused the files produced before him and directed the concerned PIO to provide the requisite information within 05 weeks time, as the officers have made the notings in their official capacity, hence, these are official records and can not be exempted from disclosure under Section 8 of RTI Act 2005. Later piecemeal information was supplied to the applicant by concerned Corps Headquarter. Applicant again filed complaint Honorable CIC for non-compliance of CIC decision. CIC showcase the concerned PIO and asked him to appear for hearing on complaint on 03 May 2011, however in the meantime, the PIO of Headquarter Corps had provisioned balance information to the applicant.

(c) Case No 3

CIC Case Ref : CIC/LS/A/2009/01109 dated 16.10.2009 and CIC/LS/A/2010/001033

Subject : Policy on withholding of DV clearance for stopping promotion of officers after their empanelment

Background

Appellant a serving officer was empanelled for promotion to the rank of Brigadier, however could not be promoted due to imposition of DV ban pending disposal of an inquiry, has sought following information from the CPIO under the RTI Act 2005.

- A copy of Policy at MS Br branch and Discipline and Vigilance (DV) Branch of Army Headquarters as exist on 14 Sep 2007 on the specific subject of 'Withholding of DV clearance for stopping promotion of officers after their empanelment" be supplied to me.

- If such a policy was not existent as on 14 Sep 2007, a clear reply 'NO' be given to me.

- If any such policy was declared after 14 Sep 2007, a copy of the same to be supplied to me, including any policies published till date, amending that policy.

- As on 14 Sep 2007, who was the competent authority at either Army Headquarter or Ministry of Defence to sanction 'withholding of DV clearance stopping promotion' for rank of a Colonel already empanelled in select list for promotion to Brigadier. A copy of the policy letter describing such an authority if in existence is supplied to me as applicable to 14 Sep 2007.

- If such a policy was not existent as on 14 Sep 2007, a clear reply of 'NO' be given to me.

- In process as described above, i.e. "withholding of DV clearance stopping promotion' for rank of a Col, is the COAS's sanction mandatory or is this decision permitted to be taken by the AG or the ADG (DV). A copy of the policy letter describing such a decisional loop if in existence to be supplied to me as applicable to 14

Sep 2007.

- As per affidavit in reply dated 18 Mar 2008 by Army to Mumbai High

Court, vigilance clearance of undersigned was withheld by competent authority of Army   on 14 Sep 2007. A copy of said file noting whereby such action was taken Army Headquarter be supplied to me. All action including stat complaint, adjudication by the Armed forces tribunal are over as on date and no investigation is in progress to deny this information.

Appellant was given the permissible and generic information, however copy of file noting relating to initiation of process leading to imposition of DV Ban could not be given because of case file contained sensitive information affecting the honour, integrity and reputation of certain serving Army Officers and others whose identities can not be revealed . Appellant preferred first appeal before the Appellate authority. First Appeal was dismissed by the First Appellate Authority stating that adequate and permissible information has already been provided to the appellant. Later appellant aggrieved with the decision on first appeal, preferred second appeal at the office of the CIC.

Deliberations

Appellant forcefully assails the stand taken by CPIO of the Army and further questioning invocation of section 8(1)(g) on the ground that disclosure of requested information will endanger life or physical safety of any person as he being officer of the Army would be last person to indulge in unlawful activity. At the same time he also assails invocation of sec 8 (1)(h) on the pretext that matter in hand cannot be said to be either under investigation or prosecution , therefore question of impediment of these process do not arise. On the other hand CPIO and officer from DV Br argued that imposition of DV Ban was initiated by certain officers and approved by competent authority and disclosure of their identity may have security implications.

Decision of CIC

CIC observed that promotional channels of the appellant have been blocked due to imposition of DV ban. This has caused severe detriment to his career progression. CIC further perused the file held with the Discipline & Vigilance branch of the Army and opined that most of the contents are routine matter and do not really attract section 8(1) (g) and (h) of the RTI Act , however revealing identity of officers may not be in the larger public interest. In the premises we are of the opinion that first two pages of the notings be made available to appellant after obliterating names and designation of officers as per section 10(1) of the RTI Act.

Compliance of Decision of CIC

As directed by the CIC, relevant extract of notings were forwarded to appellant after invoking section 10 of RTI Act, however there had been a delay in provisioning of information which was condoned by the CIC after persuasion by the CPIO.

(d) Case No 4 :

CIC/WB/A/2007/00636-SM dated 20.05.2007

Subject : Copies of Court of Inquiry, Post-mortem report, FIR, Inquest Proceedings, forensic, histo-pathalogical & ballistic reports of son (officer) died in an operation area.

Background

Applicant mother of a late Captain of the Army; her son died while serving in an operation area in J&K in mysterious circumstances. She sought copies of court of inquiry, post-mortem report, FIR, Inquest proceedings, forensic report, histo-pathological & ballistic report. CPIO transferred the case under sec 6(3) of the Act to Public Information Officer of concerned formation headquarter. The PIO of the formation HQ denied provisioning of information on the pretext that appellant is not entitled/authorized copy of the disciplinary proceedings being not subject to the Army Act in terms of Army Rule 184. Aggrieved with the decision she filed complaint to the CIC besides approaching the Raksha Mantri.

Deliberations

The CIC overruled the contention of CPIO and said that as per section 22 of the RTI Act 05, RTI Act has an overriding effect on all other enactments. Thus, irrespective of any restriction imposed by Rule 184, the information is not debarred to a citizen. He thus directed CPIO to provision available information to the appellant. At this stage PIO of concerned Corps HQ intimated that since RTI Act 05 is not applicable in the state of J&K, it is regretted that information asked for under the said act can not be provisioned to you. Appellant filed another appeal to the office of the CIC, wherein CIC directed to provision information sought. However authorities at headquarter Command in consultation with the Army Headquarters filed a writ petition at Delhi High court challenging the decision of the CIC. Delhi High court granted stay on the decision of the CIC. Meanwhile Army Headquarters alsohad written an advisory note to concerned corps headquarter to provision information sought since stance taken is not appropriate and may not be held good in the court. Later two similar cases were scheduled for hearing at Delhi High Court. The Honorable Court ordered the Army to provision the requisite information within 15 days and stay on applicability of RTI Act to the units located in the State of J&K was vacated.

Compliance of Decision of the CIC

Concerned HQ Corps has provisioned all documents sought by the mother of martyr and directed by the CIC.

Chapter 8
Implications of RTI Act on Armed Forces

General

The Right to Information Act (RTI Act) 2005 is a relatively new initiative under the democratic dispensation of our nation and is aimed at strengthening the society through free dissemination of here to fore confined information, to all citizens. Implementation of this act has promoted awareness, transparency of public schemes, highlight accountability of the governing machinery and curb dubious practices, thus increasing the overall efficiency of the administrative as well as the executive systems. It is therefore important that the provisions of this Act are applied with due diligence in letter and spirit of its conception. Indeed, there will be many occasions when unscrupulous elements would attempt to subvert this path-breaking initiative for personal gains or to promote vested interests. These aberrations will have to be taken in the stride and not allowed to retard progress on the overall positive aspects of the implementation of the Act.

The basic feature of the Act is that it specifies that all information that may be given to the parliament might also be given to any citizen who seeks that information. Inter alia, this leaves hardly any org related information that may not be made available to someone who seeks it. This feature should thus be adopted as fundamental guidelines in Army while implementing this Act. Of course, there would be information which must be restricted or denied in order that the larger interests of the state, the society or the system are not damaged, the environment is not polluted or that any one group or individual does not secure undue advantage at the cost of the others. Provisions to accommodate such restrictions have adequately been made in the Act. Point to note is that many of these facts would remain classified only for a specified period, and therefore be dealt with accordingly.

Applicability of RTI Act to Armed Forces

Once RTI Act 2005 came into effect wef Oct 2005, more and more citizens having grievances or genuine requests started approaching Army headquarters for information under the RTI Act 05. Efforts were undertaken in the past by services to include IA, IAF and IN in the second schedule of RTI Act, thereby exempting services to be out of the said Act like few organisations as given at section 24 of the said Act. Towards this, initially a case was also taken up with the Government to consider including of services in the second schedule which was turned down by meetings of cabinet secretaries. Later in the year 2008 case was again taken up by then Chairman, Chief of Staff Committee with honorable Raksha Mantri, however issue remained unsettled, thereby making said Act applicable to Armed Forces.

Obligation of Pub Auth

As per sec 4 of RTI Act every pub auth has obligation to notify/host information on to the notice boards, website etc. It is mandatory for public authorities to declare information suo motu to keep citizens informed about their activities. Of late office of the CIC has also requested all Central Government Departments to lay emphasis on obligations given out in section 4 of the Act and meet the laid down requirement. However it is noteworthy that not much progress on in this key issue has so far been made by public authorities.

Hosting of Information on Internet The RTI Cells of three services at Integrated Headquarters of Ministry of Defence has been functional, in some form or the other, ever since the Act was promulgated, and has gained considerable experience in handling RTI applications and issues related to the Act. It is essential that important information containing policy matters, circulars, routine administrative decisions etc be hosted on the Internet with a view to enable access of citizens seeking to approach under the said Act. Armed Forces being sensitive organization may keep section 8 (1) (a) of the Act in mind and only host generic information on to their Websites. By such disclosure, public will have minimum resort to use of this Act to obtain information and also further reduce unnecessary and avoidable correspondence with the public authorities.

Impact of RTI Act

Increase in the Workload One of the major implications of enactment of said Act has been incredible increase in number of applications thereby causing unexpected swell in the workload at the RTI cell and associated offices of services where from voluminous nature of repetitive information is sought by public time and again. The aspect is clearly evident from trend of cases earlier brought out at chapter V of the paper. Almost seven years have elapsed since the RTI Act 05 has come into effect; hence the awareness about it is rapidly spreading amongst the citizens. Armed Forces will have to revamp their RTI organisation at various level to deal with the onslaught and associated challenges.

Information on Personnel Issues Large number of information seekers are ex serviceman seeking information related to personal issues of retired personnel concerning their settlement of Pension and Retirement benefits. Also there are ex-servicemen or their dependants keep pursuing with their custodian of documents i.e. Record offices and Manpower/Personnel Directorate respective service headquarters about details of policies related to pension issues including family pension, disability pension and various one time grants. Hence Personnel directorate/branch of three services need to expeditiously undertake necessary reforms and host maximum policy decisions, rules and regulations on to their websites on Internet. With a view to keep citizens informed on variety of issues and curb unnecessary correspondence under the garb of RTI, that some generic nature of information pertaining to Personnel Services (PS) of three services has already been hosted on to their respective Websites.

Forecast of Vacancies of Selection Board After pursuance from large number of appellants seeking information on vacancy pattern and authority for distribution of these vacancies to various Arms/Services while undertaking promotional boards by the MS branch of the Arm, of late started MS branch in most of the cases are hosting such information on to the Intranet before the board assembled for the information of environment.

Misuse of RTI Mechanism As enumerated earlier while discussing case studies, there are appellants, who indulged in seeking information repetitively; forward frivolous applications with several vague queries, unnecessary correspond with CPIO time and again. Generally such person seeks information which does not qualify to be valid information as given section 2(b) of RTI Act. In few cases, aim of such appellants is to harass public authority or to settle score personally with officials involved. This category of applicants can easily be identified by the PIO and a complaint can be forwarded to CIC under intimation to appellant that no correspondence be undertaken till CIC decides on the case. Also some of the common example of invalid applications are enumerated in succeeding para.

RTI - Not a Grievances Redressal Mechanism RTI Act has been enacted to promote transparency and accountability in the functioning of public authority but certainly not a mechanism to address grievances. Every organisation has a well laid out system to address grievances of individuals and accord redressal, however few citizen use RTI mechanism for airing their grievances which puts extra burden on PIO. It is appropriate for the PIO neither to accept such communication and nor to treat it as a valid RTI application but if feasible, PIO may forward it to concern branch/section to look into issues and dispose it off as deemed fit.

Clarification/Explanations – Not under RTI   Also, it has been observed that few appellants seek information which per se do not construed as information given out at sec 2(b) of the RTI Act. Clarifications/ Explanations/Justifications are the role of adjudicate authority; hence PIO will not be able to respond to such queries at his own. Such applications forwarded by appellants to CPIOs are liable to be invalid and may be rejected.

Settlement of Claims RTI is not a tool to settle outstanding issues related to claims, pension, adjustment of part II orders, fixation of pay etc. Such cases are to referred to competent authority for necessary settlement and allowance. Few genuine appellants seek progress on such cases which is in order and a valid RTI query.

Allegations against Superiors Though exceptional but in some cases it has been noticed that few appellants use derogatory and threatening language or allege their superiors while forwarding applications for seeking information. If in case permissible information is asked, may be given, however appellant need be politely advised to restrict only to seeking information, airing such views are not warranted because nothing much can be done on his allegations with in frame work of RTI Act 2005.

Outcome of RTI Cases – key Decisions

In succeeding para, few policy matters are illustrated which have been given out by the CIC as decisions after prolonged persuasions in various cases and may be referred in future as when need arise.

Confidential Reports of Service Personnel As has been brought out earlier through numerous RTI cases and decisions of the CIC thereof, the CR of service personnel is debarred from disclosure under RTI Act 2005. Hence events which involve CR grading directly or indirectly are not disclosed to information seekers under the said act. Few examples are Selection Board proceedings for promotion, Nomination of officers for courses like National Defence College, Higher Command, Higher Defence Management, Senior Command, Selection of officers for foreign assignments, Proceedings of Departmental Promotion Committee (DPC), Board proceedings for the award of honorary ranks etc.

Disciplinary Proceedings - GCM and C of I There have been number of appellants who sought copies of disciplinary proceedings like Court Martial , Court of Inquiry, Summary of Evidence etc held in the past. Matter was deliberated in number of cases taking into account the Army Act and RTI Act 2005. In case said proceedings have not been concluded i.e. competent authority has not yet confirmed, it means the process of investigation not yet over, hence as given out at sec 8(1)(h) of the Act which says information which would impede the process of investigation or apprehension or prosecution of offenders can be denied , said copies are not given under the RTI Act 2005. However in case the process is concluded in its entirety, information can be supplied to information seekers, keeping in mind sec 11 of the Act.

Posting and Promotion   From time to time applications are flooded at the RTI Cell seeking information pertaining to various Selection Boards/ Departmental Screenings being conducted by the MS branch or by personnel branch of the three services. Some of the officers and PBOR who have not made it to next rank, they repetitively seek information which is either closely related to their own promotion cases or in some cases others also. The trends of such cases are on the increase. Few serving personnel of the organisation can be responded stating that Military Secretary Branch and Record offices are hosting extensive information on to the Army Intranet, which could be referred by them before invoking RTI mechanism.

Registered Welfare Societies After protracted pursuance in number of cases with the Central Information Commission, as on date following organisations of the Armed Forces which are not substantially financed through public funds and are not treated as Public Authority as defined in section 2 (h) of RTI Act; remains out of purview of the RTI Act 2005. These organisations are:-

(a)   Army Welfare Housing Organisation (AWHO)

(b)   Army Welfare Education Society (AWES)

(c)   Army Group Insurance Fund (AGIF)

(d)   Army Wives Welfare Association (AWWA)

Besides above, regimental institutions like Messes, Clubs, Unit Run Canteens (URCs) and all misc regimental activities which are established solely for the welfare of Army personnel and wherein no public funds are invested or substantially financed, remains out of the purview of RTI Act 2005, hence not mandatory to provision information pertaining to these activities.

Medical documents to Next of Kin/Parents There have been stances wherein next of kin or parents have sought for medical documents of either deceased or alive personnel. Initially there has been denial in very few cases on the pretext can not be given to anybody else than self only, however these are been made available to next of kin or parents under the said Act.

Weightage to Course Grading in Quantification Method MS branch of the Army have introduced quantification method for selection of officers to next higher rank which is promulgated and implemented. There have been frequent queries raised by large number of officers on quantification of various courses and their weightage accorded in the selection board. This information has so far not been provisioned. While defending a case at CIC the reasons given were large number of courses are conducted in the Army and quantification of each course is complex. Also such disclosure may lead to lack of interest of personnel to undergo a particular course which either has no weightage or very less. Hence in the organizational interest it is better if not revealed. The argument put across by Army was upheld by the CIC, accordingly not been provisioned under the RTI Act.

Performance in Entrance Test Performance of a candidate in the written entrance test for admission to Military/ Sainik Schools is provisioned to information seekers, however information shall either pertains to self or of their ward only. Recruiting Directorate of the Army have recently promulgated policy for provision of photocopy of answer sheets to candidate appeared for written test conducted for recruitment in to the Army for subjective examinations. The stipulated condition is that copy of answer sheet is to be asked by candidate himself for his own performance with in 45 days of conduct of the exam and also on payment of Rs 100/-. For common entrance test which is conducted for recruiting Soldiers General Duty (GD) through computerized method ie OMR (Optical Mark Recognition), facility to seek copy of answer sheet do not exist. This is not being considered viable as no human factor is involved in the evaluation.

Functioning of Army Schools Though Army Schools are under Army Welfare Education Society (AWES) which is a registered society meant for the welfare of Army Personnel. Since AWES is not substantially financed directly or indirectly by funds provided by the appropriate Government hence is beyond the purview of RTI Act 2005. However information on day to day functioning and administrative aspect is being provisioned by the AWES, however discretion whether to provision or not entirely lies with MD, AWES.

Utilisation of Grants All documents pertaining to utilization of grants, financial transactions, tendering action and inventory etc are required to be provisioned to information seekers once the contract is concluded or tendering action is completed and supply orders are placed.

Applications preferred by Advocates   Of late, numbers of Advocates are seeking information on behalf of their client by producing Power of Attorney or Vakalatnama. In a recent judgment it has been ruled by the CIC to treat such cases as third party information and be processed accordingly.

Cases received from office Bearers   As per section 3 of RTI Act 2005, only citizen of the country has right to seek information that means it is an individual right. However if an application is received duly initiated in the capacity of an office bearer of any association/societies/NGOs, the information sought be provisioned.

Areas of Concern and Suggested Measures

Lack of Knowledge amongst Public Authority Though RTI Act has been implemented wef 2005 however there are sizeable number of officials who are not well versed to deal with the cases in an appropriate laid down manner. In Army, with a view to assist Public Information Officers appointed at various formation headquarters, numbers of interactive sessions cum workshops have been conducted in the past and also environment was sensitized through issue of number of guidelines and advisories on RTI Act and related issues. Some amount of training on RTI Act could also be considered to be included in the curriculum of courses being conducted in the Armed Forces.

Inhibition of Sharing Information Armed Forces, habitually have not been sharing information, as main role of Armed Forces is related to operational and to safeguard against National Security and Sovereignty. If at all information is shared, it is need based. As regard to security and sovereignty of the nation, this aspect has been well taken care of in the Act by allowing exemption as per section 8 (1) (a) of the Act. However going through the kind of information sought by most of the appellants, it is apparent that information is usually asked pertains to routine administrative issues or in few cases related to tendering action/financial dealings. Denial of such nature of information is utter disrespect to the Act and PIOs are liable for strictures/penalty by the monitoring agencies.

Another major hurdle in provisioning of information by the CPIO/PIO is custodian of information generally feels why to share information which is closely associated with his day to day dealings, hence reticent of exposing his work. Such inhibition on the part of staff officers is unwarranted and need to be tackled by Commanders/Head of branches at all levels by spreading awareness of the Act and also bring in change in the mindset of such officials.

Discontinuity of PIOs Besides lack of knowledge amongst the officers deputed to handle RTI related issues while discharging duties of PIO; there are instances when PIOs are changed frequently by formations which results into waste of expertise gained. Some amount of continuity is required to understand the subject better and effectively tackle the RTI mechanism.

Duties performed by First Appellate Authority   As covered earlier, First Appellate Authority (FAA) generally a senior officer in the hierarchy, may be number two of the establishment and is responsible for promoting transparency in the organisation. FAA also requires overseeing effective and smooth implementation of the Act at his establishment. FAA has quasi judicial powers to dispose off appeal. Hence, officers entrusted with this assignment need to ensure that permissible complete and correct information in laid down time frame has been provisioned to appellants. For assistance it would be beneficial for FAA to refer to guidelines issued by the DOP&T vide their letter Number 1/3/2008-IR dated 25 April 2008 which can also be downloaded from their website on the INTERNET.

Misc Issues

Applicability of RTI Act 05 for Armed Forces in the state of J&K   As per Section 1 of Chapter 1 of RTI Act 2005, the Act extends to the whole of India except the state of J & K. Based on the aforesaid, initially unit/ formation Headquarters of the Army located in the state of J & K were deemed to be out of the purview of RTI Act 05 and accordingly, information seekers under the said Act were not provisioned the information held with or pertaining to unit/formation located in the state of J & K. However, CIC overruled this plea taken by Army authorities since Armed Forces are Central Government Organisation and are working directly under the Ministry of Defence. As discussed earlier in one of the case study, the stance of Army was negated by Delhi High Court in their judgment who has categorically asked Army to provision the information sought to the appellant. Hence units/formations Headquarters of the Army located in the state of J & K are very much under the gambit of RTI Act 2005 and information seekers can seek information from the respective Public Information Officers.

Conclusion

The RTI Act has had, and continues to have a significant positive impact on democratic governance in India. This is because the Act has been owned by the common people. The prime mover of the Act is the ordinary person. The Act has, in one stroke; delegitimized the norms of secrecy imposed by a colonial and feudal past with its continued legacy in independent India. Equally significant has been its capacity to empower those who use it by changing power relationships between the ruling classes and citizens. Today it has become the most important means by which ordinary people can fight corruption and the arbitrary use of power. While there are obvious shortcomings in the Act and its implementation — a fundamental transformation from a culture of secrecy to one of complete openness is still a long way off — nevertheless, in its short history, this Act has built the basic architecture of a transparent regime. But seven years after its enactment, has the RTI Act fulfilled its objectives? Has it been empowering for the common people? Answers to some of these questions are critical since these are some of the indicators for claims made by the Government.

Prime Minister Manmohan Singh while addressing at the recent convention of the Central Information Commission wherein he has openly expressed views in favour of privacy while dealing with RTI and raised three specific issues: frivolous and vexatious applications, privacy, and exclusion of public-private partnerships (PPP). These have raised concerns amongst the NGO and RTI activist that attempts are being made to dilute the spirit of the RTI Act and limit its use. Talking about this development, one of the main mover of RTI Act Aruna Roy assisted by Nikhil Dey, share their worries as

"The RTI Act needs all the support it can get. Yet, it is unfortunate that the Prime Minister repeatedly speaks of irritants when these have been addressed and allayed several times. At a time when its detractors are looking for helpful signals to dilute the Act, we had hoped Dr. Singh would celebrate the Act as an achievement and promise stronger implementation towards building a transparent and accountable democracy. While the Prime Minister did mention in passing that the RTI has strengthened democracy, the focus was on areas of concern. There have been attempts, primarily through amendments to rules, to keep out "frivolous and vexatious" applications. Since neither can be objectively defined, any such amendment will result in huge rejection, affecting mostly the poor and the marginalised. This issue has been repeatedly deliberated. The Department of Personnel and Training dropped the amendment move after its website was flooded by adverse comments. The National Advisory Committee too has rejected the amendments. The law has adequate provisions under Section 8 to reject applications that are not legitimate and Dr. Singh does not qualify why the exemption for privacy under section 8(1) J is inadequate to protect personal privacy. Nor has the government laid out those cases in which personal privacy has been infringed because of the RTI Act. The Prime Minister referred to Justice A.P. Shah's report on privacy. However, it is our information that this report has recommended that any privacy law should be in harmony with, and subject to, the RTI regime. As for excluding the PPPs, this is absolutely unacceptable, as more and more essential public services are being outsourced to the private sector. In such cases, they should be held to a higher standard of transparency as the private sector can easily escape the accountability provisions of the public sector. In fact, many ordinary people see the PPP as a ploy by the government to escape its responsibilities and accountability."

The Supreme Court, in a recent judgment, has mandated two Commissioner-Information Commission benches with the additional caveat that one commissioner must be a judge or judicial officer. Responding to this Aruna Roy said

"There is no doubt that there were many legitimate complaints about the functioning of the Information Commissions and Commissioners. The appointment process is certainly opaque and non-consultative. To begin with, the government has a 2-1 majority in the selection committee which enables it to push through a nominee of its choice. Second, while the spirit of the Act calls for commissioners across sectors, the majority of commissioners appointed have been former bureaucrats. The RTI campaign had suggested that a nominee of the Chief Justice be on the appointment committee along with the Prime Minister and the Leader of the Opposition. The RTI law does not prescribe a process of appointment. Nor has the government framed rules to address the issue. So, it would have been of great value if the court had rectified the defect by suggesting or mandating a transparent and consultative process. This was a great opportunity before the court. But the solution it has offered only creates more problems. A big problem with the commissions was mounting pendency and delays. This judgment will have the immediate effect of at least doubling this delay. Another problem was the absence of standards and norms and the judgment has failed to address that lacuna. Work has halted in many commissions. If the Supreme Court's orders are followed, all commissions may have to stop work. The Central government has filed a review petition, and the State governments are disinclined to begin the process of selecting individuals with judicial backgrounds. Chaos prevails."

If the commissions become courts of sorts, there is a danger that the common RTI user will be forced to hire lawyers to argue his case which will defeat the purpose of the Act. The commission was designed to be citizen-friendly. Judicial procedures will usher in a judicial mindset. While this may be very important in administering justice in criminal or civil law, it may defeat the quick and effective delivery of information. The custodians of information who can hire lawyers will benefit, and the ordinary will be placed at a disadvantage. Further the judiciary claims that the exceptions under section 8 of the Act can better be decided by judicially-trained mind when information ought not to be disclosed. So, from a situation of not getting enough information may result into a situation where information will be routinely denied. That is certainly a very troubling aspect of this judgment. The emphasis seems to be on the "exemptions." The RTI Act has a clear presumption towards disclosure, and even the exemptions contain a proviso of a public interest override. Actually only about five per cent of the cases go up in appeal to the commissions. But, the commissions set the tone for compliance. This judgment could pass a message not only to information commissioners, but also to Public Information Officers that a more liberal use of the exemptions under the Act would be permissible.

It is undisputed fact that RTI Act 2005 was brought into operation with basic objective to facilitate all Indian citizen to have greater and more effective access to information under the control of public authorities in order to promote transparency and accountability in the functioning of public authority. To achieve this, Armed Forces have put in great deal in setting up RTI mechanism for provisioning of information asked by the citizens of the country. The satisfaction level of citizen seeking information has been very high and is evident from number of appeals raised by the appellants. Only 13-14% of total appellants who have sought information from CPIO of Army; have filed first appeal with the First Appellate Authority and only 4-5% have filed second appeal at the office of Central Information Commission. Armed Forces initially was opposed to implementation of such act and requested government to consider inclusion in section 24 of the Act as being done for the organization like CRPF, BSF and Assam Rifles. However, once entrusted with the responsibility of administrating RTI mechanism in the Services, the commitment in meeting the aspiration of citizens is very high. The RTI mechanism established by three services have persistently monitoring RTI related activities in their respective services i.e. to conduct training, continuously afford guidance and advise on complex RTI cases. Also to render assistance to PIOs of subordinate formation headquarter to suitably defend cases listed for hearing at the office of CIC.

There have been many remarkable actions initiated by Services to provide all possible information to citizens with a view to promote transparency and be more accountable to public. Such initiatives have been acknowledged by sizeable number of appellants and also by the office of CIC. In a particular case, office of the CIC directed a Central Organisation to see the methodology of maintenance of Records undertaken by the RTI set up of the Army Headquarters and if required implement few for their department. However, at times it is noticed that some officials are reluctant to provision information or resist the natural tendency of being apprehensive of change. As per section 5 (4) and 5(5) of the Act, it is mandatory for officials to render all assistance to PIOs, else such officials can be made as deemed PIO and be accountable in case of cognizance is taken by the CIC at a later stage. It must be appreciated that by sharing information, besides transparency, correct practices and procedures are followed and one functions in more upright and methodical way. Also, RTI mechanism is overall working as a deterrent in the mind of public authority to strictly follow laid down rules and regulation and avoid dubious means and corrupt practices in their functioning. Such apprehension in the mind of officials working at various levels, definitely works positive for overall growth of the organizations.

As observed last two three years, there have been scams, faulty practices and procedural errors unearthed in the functioning of Government Departments through RTI mechanism by citizen/activists/NGO. Hence RTI instrumentality is rapidly growing and shaping into one of the best people's friendly means and also, it has become one of the key indicators for Government to claim good governance. Of late officials have suggested to the government for the review some of the limitations of the Act, however as of now no change has been accepted. Also, in the recent past there have been instances come to the fore wherein some individuals have sent numerous applications seeking diverse information, trivial/objectionable documents/ private and personnel unwanted information under the garb of said act with the aim to settle score or to harass the public authority. Indeed it known that due to their avoidable persuasion, PIO/AA have to devote most of the time to respond to their query/appeal/complaint etc at the cost of organisational interest and resources. But act of few such people should not be hurdle for PIO to respect the spirit of Act, as brought out earlier such personnel can easily be identified and can be prevented for misusing the RTI mechanism by appealing to the CIC. But no way such action by few shall hinder the latter and spirit of the Act and its efforts in implementation undertaken by organization or to retard progress made so far.

NATION

'PM's remark will demoralize people on RTI use'

Jolt to CBSE over flip-flop on RTI Act

Facing crunch, corporations push RTI offline

Not just the online facility, even the manual process of filing RTI applications has become difficult. At present, people have to go to citizen service bureaus to file RTIs

RTI shouldn't hit govt work: PM

RTI panels headed by people who've been close to govt: SC

Dhananjay Mahapatra | TNN

New Delhi: The Supreme Court on Thursday said it had directed appointment of retired judges as heads of Information commissions at the Centre and state level to ensure their independence as many were headed by persons who "have been in the good books of government".

"You will find the chief information commissioners, both at

> Not under govt, P 18

the Centre and state level, are persons who have been in the good books of the government. When these persons get appointed, and when information is sought mostly against the governments, you see the orders. They must act independently," a bench of Justices A K Patnaik and Swatanter Kumar said.

"If the Right to Information Act is to be

given some meaning, then the authorities (information commissions) must be independent in letter and spirit. But if the head of the commission is choosy about giving information on the persons who have appointed him, then it is meaning less," it said.

It entertained the Centre's petition seeking review of its September 13 ruling but not before clarifying that the judgment was aimed to ensure independence of the commissions under the RTI Act and not to rehabilitate retired judges. It posted final hearing on the petition on November 29. The bench made no attempt to hide its disappointment at the "unfair" criticism of the judgment that it indirectly aimed to rehabilitate retired judges. In turn, the bench criticised appointment of "government-friendly" bureaucrats as heads of information commissions.

SC order halts RTI hearings in 25% of panels

More States May Stop Proceedings

Himanshi Dhawan | TNN

New Delhi: The Supreme Court's order mandating the appointment of a judicial member and an expert to hear RTI-related cases has crippled the functioning of one fourth of the country's 30 information commissions.

Work in the information commissions in Arunachal Pradesh, Assam, Haryana, Jharkhand, Madhya Pradesh, Maharashtra, Punjab and Rajasthan has come to a halt, frustrating thousands who

> Case for review plea, P 21

have filed RTI pleas to fight against injustices by authorities and for delivery of basic services. These information commissions ceased working on the advice of advocate generals and legal departments of the respective states.

A survey conducted by the Commonwealth Human Rights Initiative (CHRI) showed that all such commissions have stopped hearing fresh applications for disclosures under RTI. Appeals against earlier orders are not being heard either.

The situation may worsen in the coming days because of indications that other informa-

tion commissions may choose to be "risk averse" for fear of running afoul of the SC order.

The Central Information Commission has continued work after seeking the Centre's advice. Commissions in Andhra Pradesh, Bihar, Gujarat, Himachal Pradesh, Karnataka and Tamil Nadu have also continued hearing RTI cases. In fact, the advocate general of Kerala has asked the state information commission to continue working.

However, RTI activists feel that the crisis may deepen. A pointer to that has come from Jharkhand, where the state information commission has halted work despite the availability of a member with judicial training. The Jharkhand commission is headed by Justice (retired) D R Shah.

INFO STOPPER

> No hearings in 8 of the 25 information commissions

> Others adopting a wait and watch policy and could stop hearings depending on the legal opinion they get

> States where RTI hearings have come to a halt include Maharashtra, Arunachal Pradesh, Assam, Haryana, Punjab, Madhya Pradesh, Rajasthan & Jharkhand

> States continuing hearings include Andhra Pradesh, Bihar, Tamil Nadu, Gujarat, Karnataka and Himachal Pradesh

---

THE TIMES OF INDIA, NEW DELHI
FRIDAY, NOVEMBER 23, 2012

'Info panels must be free of govt control'

Dhananjay Mahapatra | TNN

New Delhi: Additional solicitor general A S Chandhiok, in a review case on information commission appointments, said as an officer of the court he felt that "time has come to say that there should be no rehabilitation of retired judges or bureaucrats".

But the Supreme Court was keen on expressing itself fully on the importance it attached to the independence of the information commissions. It felt that adjudication requests under the RTI Act had many legal fallouts, requiring the heads of information commissions to have some legal background.

"These bodies have to be independent of the government and public authorities. The idea behind the judgment is not to rehabilitate chief justices of the high courts or Supreme Court judges. The idea is to bring in independence to these commissions. Unless you (the governments) have a problem in appointing independent persons," the bench reiterated.

When Chandhiok said persons other than retired judges could also be independent, the bench said, "But there appears to be a need for some

legal background in addition to inherent requirement of independence of the top man. We are not concerned with the rehabilitation of Supreme Court or high court judges. We are concerned with independence of the information commissions."

Rajasthan government's additional advocate general Manish Singhvi said the state has also challenged the September 13 judgment as it had made it difficult for the government to find retired judges to fill vacancies in the state information commission resulting in complete stoppage of work. The bench agreed to hear Singhvi on November 29 but said the September 13 judgment was to operate prospectively and it was wrong on the state government's part to create an erroneous impression that the judicial mandate had brought work of the information commission to a standstill.

In the review petition, the Centre had pointed to the fallacies in the Supreme Court's judgment. In Namit Sharma's case and said it was settled principle that the court could not direct the legislature to amend the law, the RTI Act, except where the law was silent on a particular subject.